ENCOUNTERING GOD TOGETHER

Almost fifteen years ago, David Peterson's book *Engaging with God* rocked my world. I had never read a book that so effectively combined faithful biblical scholarship with a passion for the gospel and linked both of them to what we call 'worship'. It remains my number one book to recommend on the theology of worship. His new book, *Encountering God Together*, is a long-awaited follow-up, providing biblical, practical, and insightful guidelines for thinking through how God wants us to meet with him as we meet with each other. He covers a broad range of topics including prayer, Scripture reading, preaching, bodily expression, liturgy, evangelism, and emotions. And as you'd expect, the beauty and power of Christ's atoning work shine throughout. Tight in all the right places and encouraging biblically informed freedom everywhere else, *Encountering God Together* should be read by anyone involved in planning or leading gatherings of the church.
Bob Kauflin, Sovereign Grace Ministries

What a breath of fresh air for our meeting with God and one another! David brings his theological insights and his pastoral longings together to help us reflect on how we do church in community. This is a wonderfully healthy and practical guide and challenge for those who lead and speak in Christian gatherings, but also for all of us who participate. To know better what we are doing and why will help us to make the very most of these times.
Paul Perkin, St Mark's Battersea Rise, London

David Peterson has done an excellent job in applying the theological framework of his earlier book, *Engaging with God*, to the practical realities of corporate worship within the life of the church. This book is fair-minded and generous, full of biblical insight and practical wisdom. Leaders of churches, congregations, preachers and musicians alike will all benefit from it.
John Risbridger, Minister and Team Leader, Above Bar Church, Southampton; Chair of Keswick Ministries

ivp

ENCOUNTERING GOD TOGETHER

Biblical patterns for ministry and worship

DAVID G. PETERSON

INTER-VARSITY PRESS
Norton Street, Nottingham NG7 3HR, England
Email: ivp@ivpbooks.com
Website: www.ivpbooks.com

First published 2013

British Library Cataloguing in Publication Data
A catalogue record for this book is available from the British Library.

ISBN: 978-1-84474-607-1

Set in Monotype Dante 12/15pt
Typeset in Great Britain by CRB Associates, Potterhanworth, Lincolnshire
Printed and bound in Great Britain by 4edge Limited

CONTENTS

ABBREVIATIONS

1QS   *The Manual of Discipline* (Dead Sea Scrolls)

AB   Anchor Bible

BECNT   Baker Exegetical Commentary on the New Testament

BNTC   Black's New Testament Commentaries

Chm   *Churchman*

esp.   especially

ESV   English Standard Version

EvQ   *Evangelical Quarterly*

ExpTim   *Expository Times*

n.d.   no date given

NICNT   New International Commentary on the New Testament

NIDNTT   *New International Dictionary of New Testament Theology*, ed. C. Brown, 3 vols. (Exeter: Paternoster; Grand Rapids: Zondervan, 1975–8)

NIDOTTE   *New International Dictionary of Old Testament Theology and Exegesis*, ed. W. A. VanGemeren, 5 vols. (Grand Rapids: Zondervan, 1996; Carlisle: Paternoster, 1997)

NIGTC	New International Greek Testament Commentary
NIV	New International Version
NTS	*New Testament Studies*
PNTC	Pillar New Testament Commentary
RTR	*Reformed Theological Review*
SBT	Studies in Biblical Theology
TDNT	*Theological Dictionary of the New Testament*, ed. G. Kittel and G. Friedrich, tr. G. W. Bromiley, 10 vols. (Grand Rapids: Eerdmans, 1964–76)
tr.	translation / translated by
WBC	Word Biblical Commentary

INTRODUCTION

I am often disturbed or disappointed by what I experience when I 'go to church'. At first glance the issues seem to be practical – poor preparation, inadequate content, inappropriate music, songs that people cannot sing very easily, uncertain leadership and superficial comments about what we are doing. Mostly, however, these practical failings seem to reveal a poor understanding of why we gather, little awareness of how to lead a gathering effectively, and an inadequate grasp of what we should expect from our time together.

Some church services proceed along well-worn paths, familiar to regular attenders, but quite strange to newcomers. Little explanation is offered about what is taking place and why it is done. There may be meaningful prayers or a challenging sermon, but overall there is something missing in the experience. At the other end of the spectrum are visitor-friendly services that are more like a concert. Each item is introduced by a 'master of ceremonies', but with no discernible flow or direction. There may be enthusiastic singing, but little else to transform the lives of the participants and equip them to serve God in everyday life.

There is little expectation in some contexts that we gather to encounter God and to be renewed in our relationship with him: church is primarily viewed as an occasion for fellowship and ministry to one another. In other contexts there is little sense of the horizontal dimension to the gathering of Christ's people: church is simply viewed as an occasion for 'worship', however that is conceived. Across this spectrum of views what we do often seems to be determined by what attracts people or makes them feel comfortable. It is easy to be driven by pragmatic, rather than biblical, concerns.

This book is written to help everyone involved in planning and leading church services think more biblically and creatively about this important ministry. Questions for review and reflection at the end of each chapter make it possible to use the book as a basis for group discussion. Pastors could especially consider using it as a training resource for those who share in the leadership of services.

We encounter God by listening to what he has revealed to us in Scripture and by responding to the work of his Son, as the gospel directs. The gift of his Spirit enables us to minister his truth to one another and to take our part in the building of his church. In biblically informed singing, in reading and reflecting on the Bible together, in biblically driven prayer and praise, and in sharing the Lord's Supper together, God confronts us with his character and will for us and makes it possible for us to submit to and serve him appropriately in every area of our lives.

This book begins by applying the biblical theology I outlined in *Engaging with God* to what we do when we gather as Christians.[1] The first chapter sets our meetings within the

---

1. In *Engaging with God: A Biblical Theology of Worship* (Leicester: Apollos; Downers Grove: InterVarsity Press, 1992) I show how the theme of worship relates to the developing story of the Bible and relates to topics such as creation, sin, covenant, redemption, the people of God and the future hope.

context of God's great work of gathering a people to himself. Worship is one way of describing God's purpose for us, and so the second chapter outlines how he makes acceptable worship possible for us through the work of the Lord Jesus and the ministry of the Holy Spirit. Chapter 3 develops the related theme of edification, showing how every aspect of our gathering should contribute to the growth and maturation of the church.

Chapter 4 examines 'patterns of service' used in traditional and more contemporary churches, and considers what might be learned from the Bible about the contents, structure and flow of our meetings. What kind of 'journey' might people experience in the outworking of a service? Why is it important that there should be a discernible order to the contributions made? Subsequent chapters deal with listening to God, praying together, praising God and singing together.

Baptism and the Lord's Supper continue to be divisive subjects, even among those who take their stand on Scripture. The last two chapters make suggestions about what could unite us in this area. They focus on what the Bible does and does not make clear. They also suggest what we might learn from the development of Christian thinking and practice after the New Testament era.

Each of the topics in chapters 4 to 10 is examined in the light of the big picture outlined in the first three chapters. Pastoral reflections arising from my own experience are included. I am particularly grateful to musicians and song-writers Brent Keogh and Mark Peterson for comments and suggestions about chapters 7 and 8.

Readers may find that certain practices familiar to them from their own church are not mentioned or are treated only briefly in this book. My aim has been to focus on things that can unite us across the churches and traditions. So the main emphases of biblical teaching and practice are discussed, with occasional reference to later developments in church history. A desire to be relevant to the surrounding culture can prevent us from discovering how previous generations of believers understood what God would have us say and do when we meet together in his name.

My prayer is that a better interaction with biblical teaching will cause those who lead congregational worship to reflect and plan and contribute more effectively. Our aim should be to honour and glorify God as we take our part in the edification of his church. But we cannot do this unless we engage more honestly and holistically with what he has revealed to us in Scripture, considering also the way Christians throughout history have responded to its challenges.

1. THE GATHERING OF GOD

'Worship' continues to be a highly controversial subject in Christian circles. For many, the issues are essentially practical and pastoral. They worry about the content and style of gatherings in their local church, constantly comparing them with what is done 'down the road'. For others, the issues are more fundamentally theological. What is the essence of Christian worship? How should a gathering be structured and led so that God's people can worship him acceptably? What are the indispensable elements of congregational worship? What is the relationship between what we do in church and the worship of everyday life?

Theology and practice cannot easily be separated. Everything we do in God's name expresses a particular understanding of his character and will, whether we acknowledge this or not. We all have an implicit theology of worship, which may or may not be faithful to Scripture. How might an authentic biblical theology of worship be expressed in our gatherings? Theological reflection is an essential step in the process of evaluating what we do together, so that we might glorify God and edify his church more effectively.

What theology of worship is implied by the following approaches?

Church A: the main aim of the gathering is to teach and exhort the congregation.
Church B: the main aim of the gathering is to encounter God in prayer and praise.
Church C: spontaneous contributions from members of the congregation are encouraged.
Church D: only a set pattern of carefully prepared prayers is allowed.

The big picture[1]

What we do when we gather as God's people ought to be considered in the light of God's intentions for us. Scripture reveals that God's eternal plan is to unite all things in Christ (Eph. 1:10). To achieve this, God is gathering to himself a vast, heavenly assembly of those who trust in his Son from every nation, tribe, people and tongue (Heb. 12:22–24; Rev. 7:9–17).

At the beginning of human history, fellowship with God was broken because of sin, and disastrous consequences followed (Gen. 3 – 11). We were separated from God and divided from one another. But God initiated a process of restoration designed to bring blessing to 'all peoples on earth' (Gen. 12:1–3). He drew Abraham and his descendants into a covenant relationship with himself, and from that context the

---

1. To some extent this section draws on the argument of a 2008 report by the Doctrine Commission of the Synod of the Anglican Diocese of Sydney, entitled 'A Theology of Christian Assembly'.

people of Israel emerged. In his dealings with Israel, God prepared the world for the coming of the Lord Jesus and the gathering of that ultimate assembly of people from all nations.

Gathering Israel

God rescued the Israelites from slavery in Egypt and gathered them to himself at Mount Sinai, describing them as his 'treasured possession' out of all nations. He promised that if they obeyed his voice and kept his covenant, they would be 'a kingdom of priests and a holy nation' (Exod. 19:3–6). That 'day of the assembly' (Deut. 10:4) was decisive and formative for the life of the people from then on. In their wilderness wanderings, and then in the Promised Land, the Israelites assembled on various occasions to meet with God, to express their devotion to him with sacrificial rituals and to respond to his revealed will with faith, praise and obedience (e.g. Exod. 29:38–46; Ps. 95).

> In the pattern of worship prescribed for Israel in the law of Moses, sacred places such as the tabernacle and temple, divinely appointed priests, prescribed rituals, and a yearly round of festivals were essential aspects of their gathering to God. Shaped by those gatherings, they were meant to treat one another with mercy, justice and love in every sphere of life (e.g. Deut. 26:1–15). Indeed, when their corporate worship did not provoke them to serve God with everyday faith and obedience, the prophets were strong in condemning the people and their leaders (e.g. Isa. 1:10–17; Amos 5:21–24; Mic. 6:6–8). They were meant to honour and serve God in every aspect of their lives.[2]

2. I have discussed this more fully in D. G. Peterson, *Engaging with God: A Biblical Theology of Worship* (Leicester: Apollos; Downers Grove: InterVarsity Press, 1992), pp. 23–49.

God sought to bless Israel by gathering them to himself, but the judgment that ultimately fell upon them for their disobedience and unfaithfulness was their scattering among the nations (Deut. 4:25–40; Jer. 11:6–13; 19:7–9). Even so, the prophets spoke of the day when God would act to rescue and restore his people, gathering them to himself once more (Deut. 30:1–3; Isa. 40:9–11), and making a new covenant with them (Jer. 31:31–34; Ezek. 36:24–28). All nations would be invited to share in this gathering, 'to honour the name of the LORD' (Jer. 3:14–18; cf. Isa. 2:1–5).

Gathering the church of Jesus Christ

In various ways the New Testament proclaims the fulfilment of those promises in the person and work of the Lord Jesus Christ. His mission was to gather the lost sheep of the house of Israel and to be their good shepherd, saving them, leading them, feeding and protecting them as God's flock (John 10:14–16; cf. Ezek. 34:11–24). More than that, in fulfilment of the original promises to Abraham his purpose was to draw people from every nation to himself (John 12:32), making disciples of all nations (Matt. 28:19). He would build his assembly or 'church', against which even the power of death would not prevail (Matt. 16:18).

God has rescued the people of the New Covenant from the dominion of darkness and death and has brought them into the kingdom of his beloved Son, 'in whom we have redemption, the forgiveness of sins' (Col. 1:13–14). Jesus our ascended high priest and saviour-king has gathered those who trust him to God's throne in heaven, where by faith we are already part of the joyful assembly that is Christ's heavenly and eternal 'church' (Heb. 12:22–24). He continues to grow this church as he sends out the messengers of his word and enables people by the power of his Spirit to respond to him with repentance and faith (e.g. Acts 2:37–42; 8:4; 9:31).

Anticipating the ultimate gathering

Christians look forward to the day of Christ's return, when that heavenly assembly will be fully and finally revealed (Rev. 21:1–4). Those gathered together by God in his new creation will continually rejoice in his victory and enjoy eternal fellowship with God (Rev. 19:1–9; 22:1–5). But even now, as believers are gathered to Christ through the preaching of the gospel and have access to the Father in one Spirit through Jesus Christ, they are drawn to each other by this new relationship with God they share. When they meet, there is a deep bond between them generated by God's Word and God's Spirit (2 Cor. 1:21–22; Phil. 2:1–2).

Every Christ-centred gathering is an expression of our union with him and with each other before God's heavenly throne. The *vertical* dimension (God's engaging with us) is primary. Uniquely among human assemblies we are gathered by God to himself, and he is powerfully present among us by his Spirit (1 Cor. 3:16–17; 2 Cor. 6:16; Eph. 2:22). So we meet with God in the presence of one another and meet with one another in the presence of God. The *horizontal* dimension (meeting with one another) is created and determined by God's approach to us. God ministers to us through the fellowship of his people and we respond to him as we pray, praise, and listen to his Word.[3]

---

3. L. Burns, *The Nearness of God: His Presence with His People* (Phillipsburg: P. & R., 2009), shows how the theme of God's presence with his people is expressed in the Bible from Genesis to Revelation. Burns draws particular attention to the transforming implications of God's presence with us through the incarnation of his Son and the gift of his Holy Spirit.

But each of our gatherings, week by week, should also be an anticipation of the ultimate assembly of God's people around his throne in the new creation. Since we await that ultimate experience of fellowship with God, Christian assembly should express an 'already' but 'not-yet' tension. We are already 'in Christ' and yet we wait to be together 'with Christ' in the new creation (1 Cor. 11:26; Heb. 10:24–25).

Christian assemblies can take place anywhere, at any time. Under the New Covenant there are no earthly sanctuaries to which we must come for worship (John 4:21–24). We, not the buildings where we meet, are God's 'house' (Heb. 3:6). A Christian congregation is God's 'temple' (1 Cor. 3:16–17), where his Spirit dwells. Jesus' promise to be present wherever two or three gather in his name should be related to this (Matt. 18:20). The risen and ascended Lord is present with his people through his Spirit, who enables us to minister to one another and to know God better.[4]

The exalted Lord Jesus Christ is the only priest we need for constant access to God (Heb. 8:1–6; 10:19–23). Our 'altar' is the cross, where Jesus shed his blood to make us his holy people (Heb. 13:10–12). Since he was 'sacrificed once to take away the sins of many' (Heb. 9:28; 10:10, 14), there are no prescribed rituals for us to follow. Worship is to be expressed in every sphere of life, as a grateful response to the saving work of Christ.

---

4. Although Matt. 18:20 and 1 Cor. 5:3–5 specifically focus on meetings for disciplinary decisions, the promise of Christ's presence can be applied to any assembly in his name. But Matt. 18:20 does not mean that any gathering of two or three believers constitutes a church. In Matt. 18:17 'the church' is clearly a larger entity than the 'two or three witnesses' mentioned by Jesus.

In view of God's mercy, we are to offer our bodies 'as a living sacrifice, holy and pleasing to God – this is your true and proper service' (Rom. 12:1).[5]

Acknowledging that we are receiving 'a kingdom that cannot be shaken', we are to be thankful and 'so serve God acceptably with reverence and awe' (Heb. 12:28).

Through Jesus we are continually to offer to God 'a sacrifice of praise – the fruit of lips that openly profess his name', and we are to express our gratitude to God by doing good and sharing with others, 'for with such sacrifices God is pleased' (Heb. 13:15–16).

Experiencing the gathering of God

God gathers his people to himself as an act of grace. So when we come together, our intentions and actions need to be shaped by God's purpose in drawing us together. Every time we meet, we need to be reminded of the basis of our relationship with God and with one another. Every gathering should be gospel-shaped. There should be an opportunity to hear again about God's character and his will for our lives, exciting various expressions of faith, hope and love.

Gathering by God's grace

The word of the gospel creates and nurtures Christ-focused, Spirit-filled assemblies. The gospel proclaims the basis on which we may relate to God and provokes thanksgiving for

---

5. I have modified the NIV translation of Rom. 12:1 and Heb. 12:28 to indicate that the Greek more literally means 'serve' or 'service'. The next chapter will explain this and show how worship terminology from the Old Testament has been adapted in the New Testament to describe the work of Christ and the response we should make to it.

all the blessings we have received (1 Cor. 1:4–7; 1 Thess. 1:2–5). God speaks to us through the Scriptures (2 Tim. 3:16–17; Heb. 3:7–11), and through Spirit-directed ministries of teaching, exhortation, and admonition to one another (1 Thess. 5:14–23; Heb. 3:12–15; 10:24–25). The 'message of Christ' may also be heard in songs that express biblical truth (Col. 3:16), in biblically informed prayer, in testimonies, in a baptismal service or in the Lord's Supper.

According to Ephesians 3:10, God's purpose is to make known 'to the rulers and authorities in the heavenly realms' his manifold wisdom 'through the church'. Ephesians 2:11–22 especially highlights the wisdom of bringing Jews and Gentiles together in one body, fulfilling God's plan to bring believers from every nation into his new creation. God's great work transcends racial, social and gender differences (Gal. 3:26–28). Our 'access to the Father by one Spirit' through faith in Christ (Eph. 2:18) is a testimony to God's extraordinary grace.

> God's wisdom is further displayed when those drawn together by the Lord Jesus love one another with the same love with which he has loved them (Eph. 4:1–3; 5:1–2). In particular, we can express that love in the way we minister to each other (1 Cor. 13:1–7; 14:26–33; Eph. 4:15). By loving one another and expressing our unity in Christ, we demonstrate that our gatherings are genuinely Spirit-led (Rom. 15:30; Gal. 5:22), and we anticipate God's new creation together.

People from every nation are called to glorify God and submit to him in worship (Deut. 32:43; Ps. 96:7–9; Rev. 14:6–7). This is made possible by the saving work of the Messiah, who draws people to himself (John 12:32; Rev. 5:9–10). Rejoicing together in his salvation, we can testify to the fulfilment of God's purpose in the Lord Jesus.

But the apostle Paul also reminds us that we need to have 'the same attitude of mind toward each other that Christ Jesus had, so that with one mind and one voice you may glorify the God and Father of our Lord Jesus Christ' (Rom. 15:5–6; cf. Phil. 2:5–11). In other words, we express who we are as the redeemed people of God by praising him together *and* by loving one another.

Gathering to express fellowship in Christ

We meet together because by God's grace we belong together. We have all heard the one gospel, received the same Spirit, and been united as members in the one body of the Son. We meet to express the fellowship in Christ that is God's gift to us. Unbelievers may be present and may become Christians because of what they hear (1 Cor. 14:24–25), but the primary purpose of the regular gathering is not to evangelize unbelievers, as I shall argue in chapter 3.

Christian fellowship is a sharing together in Christ and the benefits of his salvation (1 Cor. 1:9; 10:16–17), not merely friendship with like-minded people. We participate in something beyond ourselves. We are always in fellowship with each other and the Father through the Spirit (Eph. 2:18), because we are all members of the heavenly assembly of Christ (Eph. 2:6). But we need to experience that fellowship in practical ways by meeting together regularly and ministering to one another (Acts 2:42–47; 11:21–26). Those who believe the apostolic witness and share in the apostles' fellowship with the Father and the Son (John 17:20–23; 1 John 1:2–3) need to confess what they believe to one another for the encouragement and strengthening this brings (Heb. 3:1–6; 10:19–23; 13:15; 1 John 4:2–3, 15).

Encountering God in the fellowship of his people shapes the nature of our relationship with God and determines the nature of our relationships as the community of Christ. We are addressed by God as a congregation of his people, and respond together in prayer, praise and submission to his will. We grow together in him and share together in the grace he bestows.

Gathering to promote the growth of the church

Christians are members of the heavenly or ultimate assembly Christ is gathering to himself (Matt. 16:18; Heb. 12:22–24). From an earthly perspective, however, the church is still growing and being built (Eph. 2:19–22; 1 Pet. 2:4–5). The Lord continues to add believers to his assembly and enables us to grow in our relationship with him and with one another. In fact, Christian assemblies require further 'building' or edification in the sense of strengthening to prepare them to meet Christ on the last day (Col. 1:28; Eph. 4:11–16).

Biblical teaching about the building of the church is so important that chapter 3 will be devoted to exploring it more fully. However, three things can be said at this point. First, many gifts and ministries are given by God to believers to enable growth and development to take place (Rom. 12:3–8; 1 Cor. 12:1–31; 1 Pet. 4:10–11). Secondly, these gifts and ministries must be exercised in love if the church is to be edified (Eph. 4:15–16; 1 Cor. 13:1–13; 14:1). Thirdly, everything that takes place in the assembly – praying, singing, exhorting, teaching, confessing, giving – must be for the strengthening, encouraging and comfort of others, not merely for self-edification (1 Cor. 14:1–19).

Gathering to worship

It is common for Christians to talk about gathering for worship and to narrow the meaning to activities such as prayer and praise. But the next chapter shows how the New Testament uses the terminology quite broadly to describe our response to Jesus and the gospel in every area of life.

The exercise of gifts in ministry to one another is certainly an aspect of the *service* we are to offer to God (Rom. 12:1–8). Moreover, Acts 13:2 describes those meeting for prayer as '*worshipping* the Lord', and 1 Corinthians 14:25 envisages that prophesying in a congregation might move unbelieving outsiders to 'fall down and *worship* God'. However, since other terms such as 'fellowship' and 'edification' can describe the purpose of gathering, it is not helpful to use 'worship' as the main or exclusive term.

One of the issues we shall need to explore is the relationship between what we do when we gather together and the worship of everyday life. As a conclusion to this chapter, however, it could be said that God's gathering activity is designed to make worship that is pleasing to him possible, both now and throughout eternity.

Summary

Ever since God called Abraham and his descendants, he has been gathering a people to himself. The rescue of the Israelites from slavery in Egypt allowed them to meet with God at Mount Sinai, where they heard the conditions for being 'a kingdom of priests and a holy nation'. They were to engage with God at the tabernacle, and later at the temple, through the mediation of priests, with sacrifices and other rituals. By this means, God would keep them in an exclusive relationship with himself. Shaped by this formal pattern of worship, they were meant to serve God in everyday faith and obedience.

When Israel proved unfaithful and idolatrous, God's judgment fell. But the prophets revealed that God would restore his people, transform the pattern of worship he had given them, and gather people from every nation to share in the life of his renewed people. The New Testament proclaims the fulfilment of these promises in the person and work of the Lord Jesus Christ.

Through his death and resurrection Jesus has achieved a rescue from sin and its consequences. Through the ministry of his Word and his Spirit the ascended Lord continues to draw people into his heavenly church and to build them up. Every congregational meeting should be an anticipation of the final gathering of believers from every nation into God's new creation. Such gatherings should enable us to prepare for and move together towards that ultimate encounter with God.

Questions for review and reflection

1. What is the implicit theology of worship in the congregation where you belong?
2. Why is it important to understand the biblical picture of God's gathering activity?
3. What practical difference could it make to our weekly gatherings to see them as anticipations of the final gathering of Christ's people in the new creation?
4. List the reasons for gathering together outlined in this chapter and rank them in importance from a biblical perspective.

2. WORSHIPPING GOD

Worship has been defined quite broadly as 'the response of the creature to the Eternal . . . an acknowledgement of Transcendence'.[1] Such a description might be appropriate for the study of human religions across the ages, but it is too vague to define worship from a biblical perspective. Scripture makes it clear that some expressions of worship, such as bowing down to images (Exod. 20:4–6) or offering sacrifices to God while disobeying him in other ways (Isa. 1:10–17), are unacceptable. Just because people are religious or do things in the name of God does not mean they are pleasing to him. God must reveal what is acceptable and make it possible for people to respond to him appropriately.

More narrowly, worship has been defined as 'the celebrative response to what God has done, is doing, and promises to do'.[2]

---

1. E. Underhill, *Worship*, 3rd ed. (London: Nisbet, 1937), p. 3.

2. J. E. Burkhart, *Worship: A Searching Examination of the Liturgical Experience* (Philadelphia: Westminster, 1982), p. 17.

This rightly acknowledges that worship is a response to God's self-revelation in deed and word, but it restricts worship to some form of celebration. Although the Bible links worship with praise in many contexts, it is also associated with repentance, submission to God's will and obedience in everyday life. The common practice of limiting worship to what we do in church – even more narrowly to praise – hinders us from grasping the full scope of biblical teaching on this subject.[3]

Nowhere in Scripture is worship actually defined. Prayer, praise, confession, sacrifice, faith, obedience, and many other terms, describe different aspects of worship. But when three key word groups are examined in different contexts, it is clear that homage, reverence and service to God are central to the concept of worship.

Homage to God

The words most commonly translated 'worship' in Scripture convey the notion of homage or grateful submission to God.[4] In general use these terms expressed the oriental custom of bowing down or casting oneself on the ground, kissing the feet, the hem of a garment or the ground, as a gesture of

---

3. G. Kendrick, *Worship* (Eastbourne: Kingsway, 1984); *Learning to Worship as a Way of Life* (Minneapolis: Bethany House, 1985), p. 32, rightly condemns a narrowing of worship to praise: 'as if the highest achievement of our whole pilgrimage on earth was to enter some kind of praise-induced ecstasy!'

4. The Hebrew verbal form *hištaḥăwâ* literally means 'bend oneself over at the waist'. It is regularly translated by some form of *proskynein* in the Greek version of the Old Testament (the Septuagint). On these and related terms, see D. G. Peterson, *Engaging with God: A Biblical Theology of Worship* (Leicester: Apollos; Downers Grove: InterVarsity Press, 1992), pp. 55–63.

respect to someone (e.g. Gen. 18:2; Exod. 18:7; 2 Sam. 14:4). In relation to God this gesture acknowledged his sovereignty, grace and power. As a response to some revelation from God or some divine action, homage was expressed to God by individuals and by groups of believers together.

> *Homage might be a spontaneous expression of an individual's gratitude to God*: 'The man bowed down and worshipped the LORD', praising God for leading him to the right place at the right time (Gen. 24:26–27; cf. Job 1:20–21).
>
> *Homage might be a corporate expression of awe and submission to God's will*: when the Israelites heard that the Lord was concerned about them and had seen their misery, 'they bowed down and worshipped' (Exod. 4:31; cf. Judg. 7:15).
>
> *Homage might be a corporate acknowledgment of God as creator and saviour of his people*: 'Come, let us bow down in worship, let us kneel before the LORD our maker; for he is our God and we are the people of his pasture, the flock under his care' (Ps. 95:6–7; cf. Pss 96:9; 100:2).

Bending over before the Lord, as a gesture of homage or grateful submission, became associated with sacrifice and public praise in Israel. In such contexts it could be a formal way of expressing devotion to or dependence on God (e.g. Deut. 26:1–11; 1 Chr. 29:20–21; 2 Chr. 7:3–4; 29:28–30; Neh. 8:6). But the gesture was meaningful only if people recognized God's majesty and holiness and desired to serve him as their king.

Sometimes, in fact, the terminology was used with other words identifying a movement of the body. Such combinations suggest that the particular terms we are considering conveyed the inward attitude implied by the gesture (e.g.

'Moses bowed to the ground at once and *worshipped*', Exod.
34:8).[5] Other word combinations make it clear that homage
or submission to God could be expressed without physical
prostration (e.g. 'they all stood and worshipped', Exod. 33:10).

In John 4:22–24 Jesus affirms that Jewish worship was based
on divine revelation and was therefore honouring to God
(v. 22). However, he goes on to declare that 'a time is coming
and has now come when the true worshippers will worship
the Father in the Spirit and in truth, for they are the kind of
worshippers the Father seeks' (v. 23). Through his cross and
resurrection God's new 'temple' has been raised up (2:19–22)
and the Holy Spirit has been given (7:37–39). Under the New
Covenant, Jesus is the means by which the Father obtains 'true
worshippers' from every nation (4:23; cf. 12:32). The Old
Testament pattern of worship was a preparation for the
way of relating to God that Jesus has made possible (see Heb.
10:1–4).

Worship 'in truth' (John 4:23) involves acknowledging Jesus
as the ultimate revelation of God (14:6) and responding with
faith to what he reveals about the Father and his purposes
(8:45; 18:37). Worship 'in the Spirit' means receiving from
the Lord Jesus the Spirit available for all who believe in him
(7:37–39).[6] Jesus is not the object of worship in John 4 but the

---

5. The first term in such references describes the gesture ('he bowed
   down') and the second explains its significance ('and worshipped'
   or 'paid homage').

6. The Greek text of John 4:23 literally reads 'in spirit and truth'.
   However, NIV (2011) has rightly interpreted this to mean 'in the
   Spirit and in truth'. Jesus has just offered the woman at the well
   'living water' (4:10), which will become 'a spring of water welling
   up to eternal life' (4:14). This clearly anticipates the offer of the
   Holy Spirit, which is expressed in similar terms in 7:37–39.

means to a God-honouring worship under the New Covenant. True homage and devotion to God are possible only for those who recognize the significance of Christ and yield him their allegiance.

> The relationship with God that Jesus makes possible is not tied to any earthly 'place' (John 4:20) or special religious ceremonies. The prophetic hope of the temple as the centre for the universal worship of God in the end time (Isa. 2:1–4) has been fulfilled in the person and work of the Messiah. The exalted Christ is now the 'place' where God is to be acknowledged and honoured. The Father cannot be honoured unless Jesus is given all the honour due to him as the embodiment of truth and the giver of God's Spirit.

The same Greek verb is used elsewhere in the New Testament to show that the Son of God himself is to be given the homage and devotion due to the Lord God of Israel (e.g. Matt. 14:33; 28:9, 17; Luke 24:52; Heb. 1:6; Rev. 5:9–14). For example, when a blind man finally comes to acknowledge who Jesus is, he says, 'Lord, I believe,' and then John says, 'he worshipped him' (John 9:38). This is a way of expressing commitment to Jesus. Even where such terminology is not employed, it could be argued that apostolic preaching aimed to bring people to worship Christ in the sense of yielding their allegiance to him as Saviour and Lord (Acts 2:36–39; 10:36–43; cf. Rom. 10:9–13).

'Bending over to the Lord' in the New Testament involves responding with repentance and faith to the person and work of the Lord Jesus Christ. Such worship means acknowledging that he is Lord and calling upon his name (Rom. 10:9; 1 Cor. 1:2; Phil. 2:9–11). Those who believe the gospel are moved to pray to him (Acts 7:59–60; 1 Cor. 16:22; 1 Thess. 3:11) and to praise him (Col. 1:15–20; 1 Tim. 3:16; Rev. 5:9–14). While it is true that such devotion to Christ ought to be expressed in everyday life situations, believers have the opportunity to acknowledge him in this way *together*, when they meet in his name.

> For example, submission to God might be expressed by his people collectively as they sing in praise of Christ. Alternatively, in response to a sermon or a word of exhortation, homage might be expressed in a corporate confession of sin, in a commitment to obedience in some specific way, or in a general prayer of rededication to God's service. Submission to God may also be expressed in intercession for others. Of course, *individuals* must express genuine homage to God if these corporate acts of worship are to mean anything. From time to time we need to be challenged about whether we are truly engaging with God in the context of the gathering.

Reverence or respect for God

Another group of terms was used to express the reverence, fear or respect due to God.[7] Different contexts show that this involved keeping his commandments (e.g. Deut. 5:29; 6:2, 24; Eccl. 12:13), obeying his voice (e.g. 1 Sam. 12:14; Hag. 1:12), walking in his ways (e.g. Deut. 8:6; 10:12; 2 Chr. 6:31), turning away from evil (e.g. Job. 1:1, 8; 2:3; 28:28; Prov. 3:7) and serving him (e.g. Deut. 6:13; 10:20; Josh. 24:14; Jon. 1:9). Sacrifice and other rituals were clearly a way of expressing reverence for

---

7. In Greek these were words based on the *seb-* stem or words in the *phoboun* group, generally translating Hebrew *yārē'* and its cognates. See Peterson, *Engaging with God*, pp. 70–72.

God, but faithfulness and obedience to the covenant demands of God in every sphere of life were the distinguishing mark of true religion in the Old Testament (e.g. Exod. 18:21; Ps. 25:14; Mal. 3:16; 4:2).

In some biblical texts a parallelism between homage and fear suggests that one can be used as a synonym for the other. For example, in Deuteronomy 6:13 Moses says, 'Fear the LORD your God, serve him only', but when Jesus quotes this text in Matthew 4:10, he says, 'Worship [literally 'pay homage to'] the Lord your God, and serve him only.' If there is any difference between the terms, paying homage to God suggests particular expressions of worship, whereas fear or reverence implies a whole pattern of devotion and respect to God.

New Testament writers use this terminology in the negative, as well as in positive ways. So Paul describes the foolishness of idolatry as exchanging the truth about God for a lie, so that people 'worshipped [literally 'reverenced'] and served created things rather than the Creator' (Rom. 1:25). But Peter encourages his readers to live out their lives in this world 'in reverent fear' (1 Pet. 1:17), and Hebrews calls upon us all to serve God acceptably 'with reverence and awe, for our "God is a consuming fire"' (Heb. 12:28–29).

Serving God

The purpose of Israel's redemption from slavery in Egypt was to serve the Lord (e.g. Exod. 3:12; 4:23; 8:1). An important set of terms refers to this 'service'.[8] When the parallel expressions

8. The Hebrew verb 'ābad, which literally means 'serve', is sometimes also translated 'worship'. When it specifically refers to Israel's service to God, it is often rendered by latreuein in the Greek version of the Old Testament. See Peterson, Engaging with God, pp. 64–70.

'to offer sacrifices to the LORD our God' (3:18; 5:3, 8, 17; 8:8, 25–29) and to 'hold a festival' (5:1) are used, it is clear that some form of ritual service was in view. The priests and Levites were appointed to lead the people in their service to God.[9]

However, it is important to note that Israel's service is related to fearing God, walking in all his ways and observing all his commands and decrees. A total lifestyle of allegiance to God was clearly required of God's people (e.g. Deut. 10:12–13; Josh. 22:5; 24:14–24). Consequently, bowing down and serving aspects of the creation or other gods was strictly forbidden (e.g. Deut. 4:19, 28; 5:9; 7:4, 16). Every temptation to idolatry and humanly devised religion was to be removed from their midst.

The service of Jesus

The New Testament adapts the terminology of sacrifice and service in *two* significant ways. First, it describes Jesus in his death, resurrection and ascension as the high priest who has offered a perfect sacrifice to fulfil and replace all the ritual of the tabernacle and temple (Heb. 8:1–6; 9:11–14; 10:5–14). The Lord Jesus enables us to approach God with confidence, as those who have been purified, sanctified and perfected by him, and to live in God's presence for ever (Heb. 4:14–16; 10:19–22; 12:22–24).

Paul similarly describes Jesus' death as 'a sacrifice of atonement, through the shedding of his blood – to be received by faith' (Rom. 3:25; cf. Eph. 5:2). Only by his sacrifice can the wrath of God be averted (Rom. 1:18–28; 2:5). Reflecting Old Testament teaching about the sacrificial system, Paul indicates

---

9. The service of priests and Levites is generally indicated by another Hebrew verb *šārat* and translated *leitourgein* in the Septuagint.

that it is God who provides the means of forgiveness, cleansing and restoration under the New Covenant (Rom. 5:8–11; 6:4–11; 1 Cor. 1:30; 6:11).

The service Jesus makes possible

The New Testament also uses service terms to describe the response we are to make to Jesus and the gospel. Paul says we are to present ourselves as 'a living sacrifice, holy and pleasing to God' (Rom. 12:1). The sacrifice in question is our 'bodies', meaning ourselves as a totality (6:13, 16, 'offer yourselves'). Christ's obedience makes possible a new obedience for the people of God. As those who have been brought from death to life through Jesus' death and resurrection, we belong to God as a 'living sacrifice'. This is further described as 'your true and proper worship' (12:1).

> More literally, the Greek may be translated 'your understanding service'. The service Paul calls for is obedience, motivated by faith in Jesus Christ and what he has done for us. Those whose minds are being transformed and renewed by God will no longer be conformed to the values, attitudes and behaviour of 'this world' (12:2; cf. Col. 3:9–10; Eph. 4:22–24). Acceptable worship is the devoted service rendered by those who truly understand the gospel and want to live out its implications in every sphere of life.

Hebrews similarly teaches that the sacrifice of Christ can 'cleanse our consciences from acts that lead to death, so that we may serve the living God' (9:14). Putting it another way, the writer says we should be grateful for receiving 'a kingdom that cannot be shaken' and 'so worship God acceptably with reverence and awe, for our "God is a consuming fire"'

(12:28–29). 'Serve' is the literal meaning of the Greek verb in both passages.[10]

Hebrews 13 outlines what acceptable service means in daily life. For example, it involves simple acts of hospitality and visiting those in need. It includes marital faithfulness, sexual purity, freedom from love of money and trusting God to provide what we need (13:1–6). Put simply, we express our relationship with God in the way we speak about him and act towards one another (13:15–16). Clearly, what we do in church should acknowledge such teaching and enable us to respond to it in everyday circumstances.

Gospel ministry and service to God

The link between ministry to others and service to God is particularly obvious in what Paul says about himself. In Romans 1:9 he indicates that his service takes place specifically in the sphere of gospel ministry. Intercessory prayer is part of it (1:8–10), but gospel preaching is the focus and goal of all his activity (1:11–15).

In Romans 15:16 Paul uses transformed worship terminology again to describe his work. As 'a minister of Christ Jesus to the Gentiles', he has been appointed to bring the benefits of the gospel to the nations. In so doing, he discharges 'the priestly duty of proclaiming the gospel of God'. By his preaching, he enables the Gentiles to offer themselves to God as an acceptable sacrifice, 'sanctified by the Holy Spirit'.

Gospel proclamation brings about the obedience of faith through Jesus Christ, which is the 'understanding worship'

---

10. It is confusing that the NIV (2011) translates the same Greek verb differently in these two related contexts in Heb. 9:14 and 12:28.

that pleases God (Rom. 12:1, my tr.). Since preaching was not regarded as a ritual activity in the ancient world, Paul clearly gives that ministry a novel significance when he describes it as the means by which he worships or serves God.

In Romans 15:26 Paul refers to the service offered by certain Gentile churches to 'the poor among the Lord's people in Jerusalem'. The service he is talking about is financial support. The Gentiles have shared in the Jews' spiritual blessings and owe it to them 'to share with them their material blessings'. Here, and in 2 Corinthians 9:12 ('this service that you perform'), the terminology refers to practical help for those in need (see also Phil. 2:25, 30). This is clearly a ministry that will glorify God (2 Cor. 9:13). Indeed, such gifts are 'a fragrant offering, an acceptable sacrifice, pleasing to God' (Phil. 4:18). So one of the ways we can serve God and please him is by using our money wisely to support the needy and promote the work of the gospel.

Adoration and action

Authentic worship embraces the whole of life, but this does not alter the fact that there is a special realization or expression of worship when we gather together as Christ's people.[11] The ascended Lord relates to us collectively and inhabits our congregations by his Spirit (1 Cor. 3:16–17; 2 Cor. 6:16–18). We encounter him through the ministry the Spirit enables us to have to one another and are challenged to express our dependence upon him, to praise him and to serve him *together*. We anticipate the worship of the ultimate gathering of God

---

11. See H. N. Ridderbos, *Paul: An Outline of His Theology* (Grand Rapids: Eerdmans, 1975), p. 486; D. A. Carson, 'Worship Under the Word', in D. A. Carson (ed.), *Worship by the Book* (Grand Rapids: Zondervan, 2002), pp. 11–63.

when we make the sort of response to Christ and his saving work that is portrayed in the Revelation to John.[12]

Miroslav Volf observes that Christian worship consists 'both in obedient service to God and in the joyful praise of God'.[13] Both of these elements are brought together in Hebrews 13:15–16, which comes close to defining Christian worship:

> Through Jesus, therefore, let us continually offer to God a sacrifice of praise – the fruit of lips that openly profess his name. And do not forget to do good and to share with others, for with such sacrifices God is pleased.

Praise can be offered to God in the fellowship of his people and in everyday opportunities to 'profess his name'. Similarly, we can share what we have, materially and spiritually, in the context of Christian assembly and in daily encounters with one another. As we shall see in chapter 7, praise is a significant aspect of adoration, though the two cannot simply be identified.

Volf describes adoration as a time when the personal fellowship with God that determines the whole life of Christians is nurtured, either privately or corporately. Adoration needs to take place along with action because God did not create us to be merely servants, but above all to be his children and friends. But adoration cannot be our supreme goal,

---

12. I have written about the way the heavenly worship portrayed in the Revelation to John should impact our lives on earth in *Engaging with God*, pp. 261–282.

13. M. Volf, 'Worship as Adoration and Action: Reflections on a Christian Way of Being-in-the-World', in D. A. Carson (ed.), *Worship: Adoration and Action*, World Evangelical Fellowship (Grand Rapids: Baker; Exeter: Paternoster, 1993), p. 207.

'because the world is God's creation and the object of God's redemptive purposes'.[14] Fellowship with God necessitates co-operation with God in his plan for the world.

Every sphere of life can be a place for meeting God in gratitude and adoration. But, because of the pressure and demands of life, we need to reserve special time for the adoration of God, 'whether it means going to the "secret place" (as Jesus advised), or spending a night in the mountains (as Jesus practiced), or gathering together in Jesus' name as a community of believers'.[15] Turning to God in adoration does not entail turning away from the world: 'it entails perceiving God in relation to the world and the world in relation to God'.[16]

So adoration and action, although distinct, are *interdependent* activities. Authentic adoration cannot take place in isolation from the world, because God is engaged in the world: 'adoration of God leads to action in the world and action in the world leads to adoration of God'.[17]

Summary
Worship terminology is used in the New Testament to describe the saving work of Jesus and how we should respond to the message of his grace. Jesus has fulfilled and replaced the Old Testament pattern of relating to God through priesthood, sacrifice and temple. Homage, reverence and service are to be expressed through Jesus, as heavenly high priest and

---

14. Volf, 'Worship as Adoration and Action', p. 207.

15. Ibid., p. 209.

16. Ibid.

17. Volf, ibid., p. 211, argues that the distinction between adoration and action 'is not a distinction between activity and passivity, but a distinction between two forms of human activity'.

mediator of the New Covenant, or directly to him as the ascended Lord. These terms describe different aspects of the response to God required in every sphere of life, but with a particular expression in the gathering of his people.

The tabernacle or temple was the focus of worship under the Old Covenant, because of the mediating role of the priests and their sacrificial rituals. But for Christians the focus is God and the Lamb in the sanctuary of heaven (Heb. 12:22–24; Rev. 5:6–14).

The following diagram shows that the key terms for worship overlap in meaning to some extent. It also highlights the fact that Jesus must be at the centre of genuinely Christian worship.

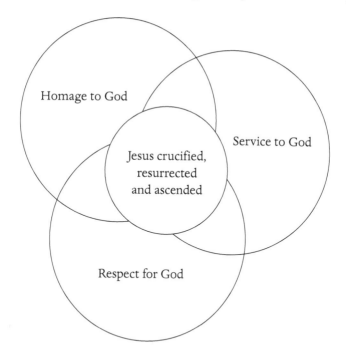

In simple terms, the pattern of acceptable worship through-out Scripture can be defined as *an engagement with God on the terms he proposes and in the way he alone makes possible.* But under the New Covenant the specific way in which God enables us to relate to him through Christ and the Holy Spirit fulfils and replaces the provisions and demands of the Mosaic Law. Acceptable worship is the expression of a genuine relationship with God. It involves individual and corporate acts of repentance, faith, praise and obedience.[18]

As we gather to express who we are as the redeemed people of God, we worship God by hearing his Word with humility and by responding with repentance and faith, in prayer and praise. At the same time, as we engage in edifying or building the church we serve God and one another, in the power of God's Spirit, for the glorification of his Son.

All ministry must be understood as a response to God's grace, and not in any sense a cultivation of his favour. Ministry to others when the church gathers is an important aspect of our service or self-giving to God. The 'vertical' and the 'horizontal' dimensions of what takes place should not be artificially separated. One part of our meetings cannot be 'the worship time' (prayer and praise) and another part 'the edification time' (preaching and exhortation), since Paul's teaching encourages us *to view the same activities from both points of view*. The following chapters will illustrate how worship and edification can be viewed together.

Questions for review and reflection

1. What new insights have you gained into the biblical teaching about worship from studying the use of the three key terms for worship?

---

18. Carson, *Worship by the Book*, pp. 26–58, offers a larger definition of worship that seeks to reflect the perspectives of both biblical and systematic theology.

2. How might we express appropriate submission and homage to God in church and in everyday life?

3. How might the service we offer to God and to one another when we gather as his people encourage us to serve when we disperse and go about our daily business?

4. How adequately do you think the definition of worship as *an engagement with God on the terms he proposes and in the way he alone makes possible* captures the breadth and depth of biblical teaching?

3. EDIFYING THE CHURCH

Any consideration of what Christians do when they meet together must take seriously the New Testament teaching about edification. Paul's instruction to the Thessalonians puts it simply: 'encourage one another and build each another up' (1 Thess. 5:11). His comprehensive teaching in 1 Corinthians 14 makes it clear that edifying or building the church should be the goal of everything we say or do together.[1]

However, it is easy to misinterpret Paul and to think of edification exclusively in terms of the spiritual advancement of individuals within the church, or to think of it as a purely intellectual activity. As with many other biblical terms, there is an important theological context to be understood before we can grasp the apostle's meaning.

---

1. The Greek verb *oikodomein*, sometimes translated 'edify' or 'strengthen', was used literally for the building of houses, temples and other structures. It was also used figuratively, for the establishment of individuals, groups or nations in some situation or way of life.

The Messiah's building work

Anticipated in Scripture

The idea of God's 'building' a people for himself is found in Jeremiah 24:6, 31:4 and 33:7, where the reference is to the re-establishment of the remnant of Israel after the Babylonian exile. To 'plant' and to 'build' go together: the opposite is to 'uproot' and 'tear down' (1:10; 24:6). God does this work by putting his words in the mouths of prophets like Jeremiah. Furthermore, he promises that if Israel's enemies learn the ways of his people and swear by his name, they will be 'established' or 'built up' in the midst of his people (12:14–17).

Amos 9:11–12 promises that this work of restoration will be done when the Messiah comes. After the exile of his people, God will rebuild 'David's fallen shelter'. In Acts 15:13–18 James quotes this passage and explains how it has been fulfilled. By raising up Jesus as the Son of David, God has begun to restore his people Israel. But Amos also predicted that God would make it possible for the rest of humanity to seek the Lord. So James observes that, in the progress of the gospel from Jerusalem to other nations, God has 'intervened to choose a people for his name from the Gentiles'.

Fulfilled by Jesus

Matthew 16:18 affirms that the Messiah will build or establish the renewed community of the people of God. Jesus says, 'You are Peter, and on this rock I will build my church, and the gates of Hades will not overcome it.'[2] Although Jesus

---

2. 'This rock' refers back to Peter's confession (Matt. 16:16), when he takes the lead in acknowledging Jesus as 'the Christ, the Son of the living God'. See J. Nolland, *The Gospel of Matthew: A Commentary on the Greek Text*, NIGTC (Grand Rapids: Eerdmans; Bletchley: Paternoster, 2005), p. 669.

speaks about his 'church' only here and in Matthew 18:17, in other contexts he indicates that the disciples are the 'flock' of God that he gathers and shepherds (Luke 12:32; John 10:11–18; Mark 14:27–28). This is another way of speaking about the salvation and renewal of God's people (Ezek. 34:11–24).

Furthermore, Jesus predicted the destruction of the temple in Jerusalem (Mark 13:1–2) and spoke about its replacement with a new 'temple' (Mark 14:58, 'not made with hands'). The false witnesses at his trial misrepresented his teaching, implying that he would destroy the existing building and build a new one in its place. But Jesus' meaning was that a new community linked to him would be established by means of his death and resurrection (John 2:19–22). 'The "presence" of God would no longer be linked with the temple, but with him and those whom he had gathered to himself (Mt. 18:20).'[3]

When Jesus tells the parable of the vineyard (Mark 12:1–12), he indicates that his own rejection by the leaders of Israel will be the means by which God establishes his purpose and builds the new community of the people of God. He makes this clear by quoting Psalm 118:22–23 ('The stone the builders rejected has become the cornerstone; the LORD has done this, and it is marvellous in our eyes'). In God's great 'building' work Jesus is 'the cornerstone'.

Acts 9:31 speaks of the way the risen Lord Jesus established his church throughout all Judea and Galilee and Samaria. After

---

3. B. Gärtner, *The Temple and the Community in Qumran and the New Testament* (Cambridge: Cambridge University Press, 1965), p. 114. See my comment on Matt. 18:20 in chapter 1, n. 4, and Nolland, *Matthew*, pp. 750–751.

the conversion of Saul, there was peace. The church was 'strengthened' (literally, 'built up') and, 'living in the fear of the Lord and encouraged by the Holy Spirit, it increased in numbers'. Numerical growth is here related to the encouraging of those who were already believers.

Acts 20:32 indicates that 'the word of his grace', meaning the gospel of grace, is the means by which a congregation is built up and given 'an inheritance among all those who are sanctified'. Human agents have an important role to play in this process, but it is clear from the theology of Acts as a whole that the ascended Lord Jesus is actually 'building' this new community through the ministry of his Word and the work of the Holy Spirit.

A community of believing Jews and Gentiles

Ephesians 2:13–22 proclaims the wonderful truth that Gentiles have now been included among the people of God. As 'fellow citizens with God's people and also members of his household' they find themselves in a new relationship with believing Jews and with God himself.

In 2:20–22 those who have been received into God's house are no longer described as its inhabitants but as the building materials of a house in which God himself dwells. The apostles and prophets are the foundation laid by God for this construction (v. 20), and Jesus the Messiah is 'the chief cornerstone'. The whole building, 'joined together' in Christ, 'rises to become a holy temple in the Lord'. Christ is the one who holds the growing temple together as a unity.

The growth of this holy temple could be in size or strength. Its growth takes place 'in the Lord' (v. 21). In other contexts Paul stresses that growth is the gift of God by using an agricultural image (1 Cor. 3:6–7) or the image of the body (Eph. 4:16; Col. 2:19). Furthermore, God's building activity is purposeful. The goal is 'a holy temple in the Lord' (v. 21), 'a dwelling in which God lives by his Spirit' (v. 22). God is progressively drawing people from every nation into that fellowship.

In summary, we may say that the plan of God is to build or establish a people amongst whom he will dwell forever in the perfection of the new creation (Rev. 21:1–4; 22:1–5). This 'construction', in which Jews and Gentiles are wonderfully united, is achieved by the Messiah in his death, resurrection and ascension, and by the consequent outpouring of his Spirit for the ministry of the gospel.

The church's building work
The ministry of apostles

In Romans 15:20 Paul speaks of his ambition to preach the gospel where Christ has not yet been named, so that he will not be building 'on someone else's foundation'. Building in this case refers to the work of evangelism. Paul considers that his commission is not to evangelize where a church has been founded by someone else, but primarily to be a pioneer missionary or church planter.

Writing to the Corinthians, Paul describes Jesus Christ as the 'foundation' of God's 'building' (1 Cor. 3:9–10). Paul himself is the 'wise builder', who lays the foundation through his evangelistic ministry, and others build on that foundation (v. 10).[4] A warning is then given about the way further 'building' takes place (vv. 11–15).

---

4. So the image here is different from that in Eph. 2:20, where the apostles and prophets are the foundation and Christ Jesus is 'the chief cornerstone'. Note also that the image of the Spirit-filled temple is applied to the local congregation in 1 Cor. 3:16–17, whereas in Eph. 2:21–22 it refers to the church that includes believers throughout time and space (cf. Eph. 1:22–23).

As 'God's temple', where God's Spirit dwells, the Corinthian congregation could be defiled and destroyed by division and quarrelling (vv. 16–17; cf. 1:10–12). In this context, building properly on the foundation laid by Paul involves encouraging one another to be united in the gospel and the traditions he delivered to them. But their ministry to one another would be effective only if it was exercised in love (13:1–13).

> In a later letter to the Corinthians Paul says the Lord gave him authority 'for building you up rather than tearing you down' (2 Cor. 10:8; 13:10). The context here suggests that building means teaching, warning and encouragement beyond the initial task of evangelism. All this is for the 'strengthening' of the church in Corinth (2 Cor. 12:19).

We may conclude that in Paul's writings 'building' is a metaphor for 'founding, maintaining and advancing' the church of Jesus Christ in his way.[5]

The ministry of gifted leaders

From Ephesians 4:7–11 we learn that the ascended Christ builds his church through the people he provides as apostles, prophets, evangelists, pastors and teachers. These ministries of the Word are critical to the process. Just as Jeremiah was told that the message given to him by God would be the means of establishing his purposes (Jer. 1:9–10), so also the church is

---

5. P. Vielhauer, *Oikodomé: Aufsätze zum Neuen Testament*, Theologische Büchere, Neues Testament, 35 vols. (Munich: Kaiser, 1979), vol. 2, p. 72 (my tr.). Cf. H. N. Ridderbos, 'The Upbuilding of the Church', in *Paul: An Outline of His Theology* (Grand Rapids: Eerdmans, 1975), pp. 429–486.

founded, maintained and advanced through the preaching and teaching of the gospel.

The purpose of the gifts listed in Ephesians 4:11 is 'to equip his people for works of service, so that the body of Christ may be built up' (v. 12). As in verse 16, where the terminology of 'building' occurs again, every member of the church is to be involved in the task of edification. But they need to be prepared for this by sound teaching and be encouraged to see how they can make a contribution to the growth of the body.

> The first phrase in Ephesians 4:12 is literally 'for the equipment of the saints'. A change of preposition in the Greek text suggests that the phrase 'for the work of ministry' is subordinate to the first one. The next phrase is literally 'for building the body of Christ'. This describes the goal of the ministry of all believers and explains why they need to be equipped or prepared properly to engage in this task. In short, 'Christ has given "special" ministers so that they will "make God's people fully qualified", thus enabling them to serve their Lord by serving one another'.[6]

The building metaphor could suggest that church growth takes place 'by substantial additions which it receives rather than produces itself'.[7] Growth by evangelism would certainly be implied with mention of the gifts of apostles and evangelists. However, by moving from the temple metaphor to the body metaphor, Paul develops the idea that the church is an organism that grows from within, by means of its own

---

6. P. T. O'Brien, *The Letter to the Ephesians*, PNTC (Grand Rapids: Eerdmans; Leicester: Apollos, 1999), p. 303. O'Brien discusses the structure and meaning of Eph. 4:12 on pp. 301–305.

7. M. Barth, *Ephesians 4–6*, AB 34A (New York: Doubleday, 1974), p. 440.

God-given life. Such growth involves maturing and strengthening, as well as growth in size.

In Ephesians 4:13 the ultimate purpose of the activities mentioned in verse 12 is outlined: 'until we all reach unity in the faith and in the knowledge of the Son of God and become mature, attaining to the whole measure of the fullness of Christ'. One goal is described by three parallel expressions. The verb 'reach' may suggest a solemn meeting with Christ at his second coming, when the church finally will be conformed to his glory (Eph. 5:27; Phil. 3:20–21; Rom. 8:29–30; Col. 3:4).

Paul's point is not to urge us to grow individually, so that each becomes perfect in Christ, nor does he simply suggest that the church must grow corporately into the likeness of Christ. The ministries given by the ascended Christ to his church (v. 11) encourage the activities mentioned in v. 12, until the people of God together meet their Lord and share in his glory (v. 13). Put another way, we may say that the purpose of Christian ministry is to prepare God's people to meet their Lord (see Col. 1:28–29).

Perfection is not an ideal to be attained by constant improvement in this life but a reality to be met in Christ (see 1 John 3:2). The goal is complete unity, maturity and Christlikeness for the people of God as a whole.

Unity has been established in Christ through the events described in Ephesians 2:11–22, and the readers are strongly urged to maintain 'the unity of the Spirit' (4:3). But in 4:13 there is a 'unity in the faith and in the knowledge of the Son of God' they still need to attain. Again, although the church is described as 'the fullness' of Christ (1:23; cf. 4:10), Paul prays that his readers might be 'filled to the measure of all the fullness of God' (3:19), and now speaks of 'attaining to the whole measure of the fullness of Christ' (4:13).

The ministry of all Christians

In Ephesians 4:12–16 the apostle begins to explain how believers can engage in 'works of service, so that the body of Christ may be built up'. Unstable, immature Christians need teachers who can lead them away from error and establish them in the truth (v. 14). Only in this way can they serve Christ effectively and reach the goal he has set for them. In this context the expression 'speaking the truth in love' (v. 15) is best taken to mean lovingly speaking to one another sound teaching.[8] The growth of the church toward Christ, who is the head of the body, takes place when his people unite in confessing the truth about him with love for one another.

It is interesting to note that growth comes from Christ (v. 16) to enable the church to grow in every way toward Christ (v. 15 recalls the imagery of v. 13). It is quite clear from verse 16 that the body literally 'makes the growth of the body for the upbuilding of itself in love'. However, it does this only because Christ is at work fitting and joining the whole body together.

So the final emphasis of the passage is on the need for members of the body to be 'rightly related to one another, each making its own contribution, according to the measure of its gifts and function, to the upbuilding of the whole in love'.[9] Edification occurs when *Christians minister to one another in word and deed, seeking to express and encourage a Christ-centred*

---

8. Barth, ibid., p. 444, observes that 4:14–15 calls for 'the right confession and it urges the whole church and all its members to be a confessing church'. Eph. 4:19, with its emphasis on the right choice of language, suggests that everyday conversation amongst believers can also be the means of building one another up in Christ.

9. R. Y. K. Fung, 'Some Pauline Pictures of the Church', *EvQ* 53 (1981), pp. 95–96.

faith, hope and love. Clearly, this ought to take place when the congregation meets together, but also as individuals have the opportunity to minister to one another in everyday life situations (1 Cor. 8:1; 10:23).[10]

Paul's focus in Ephesians 4:11–16 is not simply on the need for individual believers to learn 'more and more to live as a part of a great whole'.[11] Use of the expression 'builds itself up in love' (v. 16) implies that they have a goal to pursue *together*. The same expression reminds us that although the church has been built by God 'on the foundation of the apostles and prophets' (2:20), it is far from being a completed house of God (2:22). Growth is required.

The body builds itself up in love only because the Lord Jesus is at work through his Spirit, joining and holding it together, providing sustenance to 'every supporting ligament' (4:16). In speaking of growth from the head towards the head, Paul is showing that there is a 'vertical' as well as a horizontal dimension to edification.

When we 'speak the truth in love' to one another (4:15), error and false teaching are avoided (v. 14). This enables the church to focus on the exalted Lord Jesus and his goals for us, 'until we all reach unity in the faith and in the knowledge of the Son of God and become mature, attaining to the whole measure of the fullness of Christ' (v. 13). Edification is all about growing together 'towards' or 'into' Christ.

---

10. Love builds up when believers regard the weaknesses of others and see the need to strengthen them in their relationship with Christ. In practical terms this may involve some restriction of personal liberty.

11. J. A. Robinson, *St. Paul's Epistle to the Ephesians* (London: James Clarke, n.d.), pp. 102–103.

Ministry when the church gathers

It would appear from 1 Thessalonians that individuals participate in the building of the church by receiving apostolic teaching (4:13 – 5:10) and then using it to encourage others (5:11). The command to 'encourage one another' is followed by 'and build each another up', indicating a close link between mutual encouragement and edification.[12]

In 1 Thessalonians 5:12–22 it becomes clear that edification involves both encouragement and warning, perhaps in the context of giving and receiving 'prophecies'. Leaders participate in this ministry (v. 12), but so do others in the congregation (v. 14). Although this ministry concerns the present life of believers, the encouragement Paul wants them to give one another is based on his teaching about the return of Christ. The church is edified by keeping constantly in view the destiny God has for it.

Ministry to one another in love

The terminology of edification occurs more frequently in 1 Corinthians 14 than in any other chapter of the New Testament. It is particularly significant in the argument about the relative value of prophecy over against tongues.[13] The context indicates that Paul's first concern is intelligibility. Being 'inspired' is not enough: when Christians gather together, words should convey meaningful truth:

---

12. The ministry of encouragement, which is the responsibility of all Christians, involves moral appeal and consolation on the basis of gospel truths in the manner of the apostle's own teaching.

13. I discuss the nature of congregational prophecy in '"Enriched in Every Way": Gifts and Ministries in 1 Corinthians', in B. S. Rosner (ed.), *The Wisdom of the Cross: Exploring 1 Corinthians* (Nottingham: Apollos, 2011), pp. 134–163.

For anyone who speaks in a tongue does not speak to people but to God. Indeed, no one understands them; they utter mysteries by the Spirit. But the one who prophesies speaks to people for their strengthening, encouraging and comfort. (14:2–3)[14]

Only speech that can be understood by others has the potential for edifying the congregation. 'Anyone who speaks in a tongue edifies themselves, but the one who prophesies edifies the church' (v. 4). Paul does not rebuke the tongues-speaker for self-edification as such but indicates that this falls short of the primary goal of Christian assembly (vv. 16–17). The apostle is opposing 'an understanding of worship as a private exercise in which individuals seal themselves off from others and concentrate exclusively on their personal experiences'.[15]

> To pursue what is beneficial for the church is to fulfil the opening injunction of 1 Corinthians 14 to 'follow the way of love' (cf. 13:13). In effect, the argument here is that 'speaking the truth in love' is the means by which edification takes place (see Eph. 4:15–16). This emphasis is continued in 1 Corinthians 14:6–17, where Paul insists that public praying and singing must also be intelligible and truthful, so that others may be able to say the 'Amen' and be edified.

Since edification cannot take place unless individuals are instructed (1 Cor. 14:19) and encouraged (v. 31), the apostle

---

14. The word translated 'strengthening' comes from the same root as the verb 'build (up), edify', which is used in vv. 4–5, 12. It would be more consistent to translate v. 3 as 'for their edification'.

15. R. P. Martin, *The Spirit and the Congregation* (Grand Rapids: Eerdmans, 1984), p. 70.

is concerned that the Corinthians should excel in those gifts that 'build up the church' (v. 12). Moreover, the very act of ministering the truth to one another should be an exercise of love: only when a church is functioning in this way can it be said that it is being edified. For this reason, Paul concentrates in 14:26–40 on the manner in which gifts are to be exercised in the congregation.

The paragraph begins with the challenge 'Everything must be done so that the church may be built up' (v. 26) and concludes with the injunction 'Everything should be done in a fitting and orderly way' (v. 40). Order, and not disorder, will be a sign of the Spirit's presence and control, since 'God is not a God of disorder but of peace' (v. 33).

Paul envisages that members of the congregation will come together prepared to make a contribution: 'a hymn, or a word of instruction, a revelation, a tongue or an interpretation' (v. 26; cf. v. 6). Only one person may speak at a time and only a certain number may speak on each occasion. The majority, including those wishing to contribute, should listen in silence and 'weigh carefully what is said' (v. 29). Listening with discernment is part of the task of edifying the congregation, even though it appears to be such a passive role! The aim of these and other controls is 'so that everyone may be instructed and encouraged' (v. 31). Note here the harmonious combination of freedom and restriction.

Ministry to outsiders

In 1 Corinthians 14:22–25 the possibility of 'enquirers' or 'unbelievers' entering the assembly is envisaged. Confronted by tongues-speaking, such people may say that those participating are mad. Confronted by everyone prophesying, such visitors may be convicted and converted, acknowledging the presence of the true and living God in the midst of his people.

Some commentators have given undue emphasis to these verses, concluding that Paul's overriding concern in this chapter is 'missionary witness', or that such potential visitors to a congregation provide for Paul 'the proper yardstick' for estimating the value of ministries.[16] This perspective is reflected in the practice of some contemporary churches, where the relevance of everything that takes place for unbelievers or enquirers is critical for the planning and conduct of services.

It is more accurate to say that the apostle's overriding concern is for the edification of the church in the sense outlined above. When believers minister to one another in love, visitors may be converted because gospel truth is being proclaimed and demonstrated before them.

Of course, churches may plan to invite unbelievers or enquirers to hear the gospel on specially designed occasions. But where the focus is on making every public gathering 'seeker friendly', the edification of the church in the sense of its strengthening and maturation must surely suffer. There may be such a ministry in other contexts, such as home groups or Bible classes, but Paul's concern here is with the gathering of 'the whole church' (v. 23).

Patterns for ministry today

People from charismatic churches tend to take passages like 1 Corinthians 14 as the main guideline for the conduct of their meetings, whereas people from more traditional churches look to passages such as Acts 2:42–47 as their model. But both approaches are too restricted when the broader evidence of the New Testament is examined.

---

16. So W. Richardson, 'Liturgical Order and Glossalalia in 1 Corinthians 14:26c–33a', NTS 32 (1986), p. 147; E. Schweizer, Church Order in the New Testament, SBT 32 (London: SCM, 1961), p. 226.

These windows into the practices of two early church communities were not given to establish a pattern for each and every gathering throughout Christian history.[17] In 1 Corinthians 14 Paul is seeking to correct the excesses of that church and to encourage a more edifying conduct of their meetings. He does not commend to any other church their particular way of doing things.

In Acts 2 Luke celebrates the formation of the first Christian community in Jerusalem and highlights the way the Spirit enabled them to relate to one another and to those who were not yet believers in Christ. But later in Acts he briefly mentions other patterns of church life (11:21–30; 19:8–10; 20:7–12) and does not apparently commend any one model over another to his readers.

The reality is that New Testament writers do not commit the various churches addressed to any set pattern for meeting together. But they regularly articulate theological principles that should govern our thinking and they provide positive examples to encourage and guide us in our practice. Many of these will be discussed and applied in the chapters that follow.

Summary
The New Testament uses 'building' terminology to talk about God's great work of establishing the New Covenant people of God. This takes place through the death, resurrection and ascension of the Lord Jesus Christ, which leads to the sending

---

17. For example, it is inappropriate to regard the four elements specified in Acts 2:42 as a primitive 'service outline', implying that their meetings regularly involved instruction, fellowship, then the Lord's Supper and prayers. Acts 2:44–47 is an expansion on this initial summary and shows that their pattern of ministry did not conform to such a simple structure.

of his representatives to preach the gospel in the power of his Spirit. Apostolic teaching is foundational for the growth, strengthening and maturation of the church, but the ascended Christ also gives other gifts and ministries to further this process.

The apostle Paul writes about Word-based ministries being given to equip Christ's people 'for works of service, so that the body of Christ may be built up' (Eph. 4:12). In various contexts, he illustrates practical ways in which believers can play their part in edifying the church. But this can happen only because the Lord himself makes it possible through the operation of his Spirit.

Paul particularly uses the terminology of edification to oppose individualism in congregational ministry. His concern is that Christians should strengthen and encourage one another in faith and love, always having in view God's ultimate purpose for his people collectively.

When Christians gather together to minister to one another the truth of God in love, the church is manifested, maintained and advanced in God's way. But even in the affairs of everyday life, as they relate to one another and to unbelievers, Christians should be concerned for the edification of the church.

Questions for review and reflection

1. Why is it important to understand God's 'building' activity in the broad terms set out in this chapter?
2. What are some of the practical implications of viewing your congregation as God's 'temple'?
3. Why does Paul change the image from 'building' to 'body' in Ephesians 4:11–16?
4. Given the teaching in 1 Corinthians 14, how could you tell if a church was truly being edified?

4. PATTERNS OF SERVICE

Most churches have a fairly predictable pattern of service, though this may vary according to the time of meeting and the theme of the day. Some gatherings change in the course of a month, providing different versions of the same pattern. Some churches are more formal than others, having a printed form of service, with set prayers and a regular order of items. This is often called a 'liturgy'.[1] Other churches may be less structured and less formal, but still follow a recognizable pattern each week.

---

1. Greek *leitourgia* literally means 'a work on behalf of the people'. Such terminology is used in the New Testament to describe the ministry that Christians can have to one another, moved and inspired by the unique work of Christ on their behalf (e.g. 2 Cor. 9:12; Phil. 2:17, 30). In time the word came to be used for the pattern of service or 'liturgy' followed in congregational ministry.

- Some have the Lord's Supper regularly and others do not.
- Some have blocks of singing at the beginning and end of the gathering, while others have songs placed strategically throughout the meeting.
- Some have contemporary music, with a variety of instruments and vocalists, while others have a more traditional offering.
- Some use visual media or drama to teach and involve people, but others do not.
- Some are led by one or two people, while others include many in the leadership of the gathering.
- Some have one Bible reading, while others have two or three.
- Some make the sermon the main feature of the gathering, while others do not.
- Some say prayers together, while others rely on leaders to pray or have times of spontaneous prayer from members of the congregation.

Evaluating patterns of service

According to one early Christian writer, a Sunday gathering in the middle of the second century AD followed this simple pattern:

> The memoirs of the apostles or the writings of the prophets are read as long as there is time. Then, when the reader has finished, the president, in a discourse, admonishes and invites the people to practise these examples of virtue. Then we all stand up together and offer prayers.[2]

---

2. Justin, *Apology* 1.67 (B. Thompson, *Liturgies of the Western Church* [Cleveland: Collins World, 1962], p. 9).

The Lord's Supper followed and there was a collection for those in need. Surprisingly, there is no mention of singing in this order of service.

Very soon, liturgies developed that were more prescriptive. They provided set forms of prayer and praise and affirmations of faith for the leader and the congregation to share as the service progressed. These liturgies varied in length, substance and faithfulness to Scripture. There is much to be learned from comparing and contrasting them.[3]

During the sixteenth and seventeenth centuries new liturgies were published by most of the Protestant Reformers, replacing medieval patterns of service. Their aim was to give free course to the reading and exposition of Scripture, to express the truths of the gospel clearly and enable believers to respond appropriately. Modern versions of these services continue to be used in some churches today. In many contexts, however, more informal approaches are common.

Different attempts have been made to classify patterns of service across the churches. Perhaps the simplest approach is to view them in terms of three organizing principles: music, preaching or table (meaning the Lord's Supper).[4] Each congregation sits somewhere in a spectrum, combining these elements in different ways. But what occupies the dominant position and why? Many churches speak about encountering

---

3. A number of historic liturgies are examined and assessed theologically by Thompson, *Liturgies of the Western Church*.

4. L. Ruth, 'A Rose by Any Other Name: Attempts at Classifying North American Protestant Worship', in T. E. Johnson (ed.), *The Conviction of Things Not Seen: Worship and Ministry in the 21st Century* (Grand Rapids: Brazos, 2002), pp. 33–51, surveys a number of different ways of classifying services.

God in corporate worship and view this as happening through music, preaching or the Lord's Supper.

In the last chapter I argued that New Testament teaching about the edification of the church is critical for evaluating what we do together. In this chapter I want to apply that teaching to the content, structure and flow of our gatherings. We encounter God and mature in our relationship with him as we minister to one another in the fellowship of his people. If the church is to be edified by the experience of corporate worship, three critical questions need to be asked about the order of service or liturgy. Each question will be explained and explored in the argument that follows.

1. Does the order contain enough of the elements that the New Testament suggests are necessary for the encouragement and maturation of Christians?
2. Does the structure, flow and content of the gathering sufficiently reflect biblical teaching about the way we should relate to God together?
3. Does the service enable God's people to minister to one another as the New Testament directs?

Gathering for encouragement and maturation
Encouragement for godly living

According to Hebrews 10:24, Christians need to 'spur one another on towards love and good deeds'. We do not simply gather for the spiritual uplift we may experience, but to encourage one another to be outward looking, to care for our neighbours, our society and our world (see Gal. 6:10). Sharing the gospel, or at least being prepared to 'give an answer to everyone who asks you to give the reason for the hope that you have' (1 Pet. 3:15), should be part of that commitment.

> *Application question*: Does the pattern of service you experience encourage the participants to love God and neighbour in everyday life situations or is it simply focused on the needs of those who gather?

Hebrews 10:25 talks about 'not giving up meeting together, as some are in the habit of doing, but encouraging one another – and all the more as you see the Day approaching'. The word translated 'encouraging' could also be rendered 'exhorting'. It is used in 3:12–13 with reference to warning people about turning away from God with hardened hearts.[5]

The writer of Hebrews describes his own work as a 'word of exhortation' (13:22), and seems to be inviting readers to follow his example in their ministry to one another. Hebrews involves a wonderful blend of encouragement and warning. It uses Scripture to explain the person and work of the Lord Jesus and focus attention on the hope he has given us (e.g. 3:1–6; 4:14–16; 10:19–23; 12:1–3). Examples of faith and perseverance throughout biblical history are used as encouragements (6:12; 11:1–40). These are linked to serious warnings about the danger of missing out on what God has promised (2:1–4; 3:7 – 4:13; 5:11 – 6:8; 10:26–39; 12:14–17).

Such a ministry might take place informally, in personal contacts between believers or in counselling situations. It could certainly feature in small group meetings for Bible study and prayer. In a larger gathering the reading and exposition of Scripture will be the main way of exhorting the congregation.

---

5. The Greek verb *parakalein* is used in both contexts and elsewhere in the New Testament. It can vary in meaning from 'comfort' and 'encourage' to 'exhort' and 'warn'. The context must determine the meaning in each case.

Reading, teaching and exhortation

Paul's instruction to Timothy is, 'until I come, devote yourself to the public reading of Scripture, to preaching and to teaching' (1 Tim. 4:13). The word translated 'preaching' here is literally 'exhortation'. Effective public ministry of the Scriptures will involve reading passages out loud, then teaching and applying the message to those present by way of exhortation.[6]

God speaks to us through the Scriptures he caused to be written and through Spirit-directed teaching and exhortation from the Bible. Sermons in our churches need to have a satisfactory blend of biblical teaching and application to those being addressed. More will be said about this in the next chapter. But, even without explanation, the Scriptures can 'make you wise for salvation through faith in Christ Jesus' and they are 'useful for teaching, rebuking, correcting and training in righteousness, so that all God's people may be thoroughly equipped for every good work' (2 Tim. 3:15–17).[7]

> In some churches, only short passages of Scripture are read. This is sometimes justified by saying that people cannot understand too much of the Bible without explanation. But this

---

6. Use of the definite article in the original of 1 Tim. 4:13 ('the reading, the exhortation, the teaching') suggests that these were three related public events, following the pattern of the Jewish synagogue (Acts 13:15; 2 Cor. 3:14). Justin, *Apology* 1.67, observed this pattern in the second century AD (see n. 2 above).

7. The expression translated 'all God's people' is literally 'the man of God'. This probably refers to Timothy as a leader of God's people. However, it is certainly true that all God's people, as well as their leaders, need to be equipped to serve him better by being trained in the Scriptures.

seems to be a denial of the Spirit's ability to illuminate the minds of those who are listening. In my experience, where substantial passages from both the Old and the New Testament are carefully chosen and well read, people learn a great deal simply from listening and reflecting. Those who read the Bible to the church need to understand the passage and be able to communicate its meaning by the way they speak. Good preparation is essential. Not everyone is good at public reading!

Of course, there are different ways of communicating the contents of the Bible to a gathering of God's people. Some passages can be read together or as a dialogue between different halves of the congregation. In a dramatic reading several people might take the part of characters in a story, with one being the narrator. With music and images, a video presentation may help people reflect on the meaning of a passage. A sermon based on an extensive portion of Scripture may involve progressive readings by someone, with the preacher commenting on each segment and finally drawing the whole together with application and prayer.

Praying, singing and testifying to God's goodness

Praying together should be a means of focusing our attention on God's concerns and seeking more effective involvement in his service. The content and style of prayer needs to be carefully considered, so that this ministry is honouring to God and edifies the church. Chapter 6 explores different ways in which this might happen.

Singing together can be both a means of teaching and admonishing one another 'with all wisdom' and an expression of praise and thanksgiving to God. In this way the message of Christ may dwell richly among his people (Col. 3:16), and

God's Spirit may minister to us (Eph. 5:18–20). Chapters 7 and 8 deal with different dimensions of this ministry in some detail.

Affirmations of faith can be valuable ways of encouraging people to respond to God together. Traditional creeds or short biblical passages read together can function as expressions of confidence in God and his promises. Although some songs have a creedal character, it is difficult to express some of the deep truths of Scripture adequately in song. Reciting familiar words together can provoke thoughtful reflection and enable response to the character and deeds of our God.

Personal testimonies can draw attention to God's grace in our lives, as we hear about the struggles of others and find inspiration in their example. Testimonies can be about the way someone became a Christian, how a difficult life-situation was transformed by God or how specific prayers were answered. One church I know had a weekly series of testimonies from congregational members about serving as a Christian in different vocational contexts. Video clips can be a convenient way of bringing someone's personal journey before the congregation.

> *Application question*: How does your pattern of service convey biblical truth and people's experience of God's grace, so as to inspire God-honouring prayer, praise and mutual encouragement?

Reflecting biblical teaching about the way we relate to God

Particular elements in a service may be helpful, but what is the impact and significance of the whole? Is there a logic that people can appreciate, or do they simply experience a disconnected series of items? Preachers who are concerned about the structure, development and impact of their sermons should consider whether they apply the same concerns to the preparation and conduct of services.

Some follow the 'hymn-sandwich' approach, where songs are used mainly as convenient fillers or bridges between disparate items. Others gear everything to the sermon, so that the same theme is heard several times in readings, sermon, prayers and songs. Some advocate a structure with its own logic that can be adapted to the theme or emphasis of any service. For example:[8]

- *The Gathering*: the people are gathered to God by prayer and singing.
- *The Word*: the people are encouraged and challenged through the reading and teaching of the Bible.
- *The Response*: the people respond to the ministry of the Word in prayer, praise and other forms of ministry to one another, and/or share in the Lord's Supper together.
- *The Sending*: the people are sent out to serve God in everyday life with some expression of dedication and/or blessing.

Those who lead services should indicate, without tedious explanation, why particular songs are sung and why prayers or affirmations of faith occur where they do. Why has the order changed this week and why has this new item been included? There may be different moods created by a call to confess sins and repent or by an encouragement to praise God

8. This is an adaptation of the structure argued by C. M. Cherry, *The Worship Architect: A Blueprint for Designing Culturally Relevant and Biblically Faithful Services* (Grand Rapids: Baker, 2010).

enthusiastically. How will the transition be managed in a way that is not artificial or manipulative? Participants should be helped to realize where the whole event is taking them, with its readings, its teaching and its responses.

A gospel logic

Each element in a service should express an aspect of biblical teaching about the way we relate to God and give us the opportunity to respond together. The sermon should not be the only moment when this happens. Whatever the theme of the day, the whole occasion should enable those present to reconnect with God and be renewed in his service. Chapter 10 considers how the Lord's Supper may function in this way. Here I want to suggest how the gospel might shape and influence every Christian gathering.

For example, the promise of forgiveness on the basis of Christ's sacrificial death needs to be heard and appropriated by believers on a regular basis. Living in the light of God's character and will demands ongoing confession of sin and calling upon God to 'forgive us our sins and purify us from all unrighteousness' (see 1 John 1:5 – 2:2). Praise and thanksgiving is sometimes associated with the assurance of forgiveness in the New Testament (Eph. 1:3–7; Col. 1:12–14). Such praise and thanksgiving are then linked with prayer for more fruitful discipleship (Eph. 1:17–23; Col. 1:9–11).

This gospel sequence – confession, assurance, thanksgiving, praise and prayer – could be experienced in the structure of a service in various ways.

> I have heard it said that regularly challenging Christians to confess their sins together and seek God's forgiveness undermines assurance in their status as those justified by faith and

> reconciled to God through Christ. But this fails to take the
> argument of 1 John 1:5 – 2:2 seriously. It is also important to
> note how Hebrews stresses that we are cleansed, sanctified and
> perfected through the sacrifice of Christ (Heb. 9:14; 10:10, 14),
> but that we should keep approaching God with confidence for
> mercy and 'grace to help us in our time of need' (4:16).

Gospel-true, heart-resonant and culturally relevant

Bryan Chapell has some valuable things to say about how
the gospel might shape our practice. He does this within the
context of observing what has happened in many churches in
recent decades.

> The search for worship that is gospel-true, heart-resonant, and
> culturally relevant has taken several turns over the last half
> century. Some movements have sought release from formalism
> and traditionalism; others have found renewed appreciation for
> ancient forms of worship that link the contemporary church to
> its primitive roots. Each has sought to unchain the church from
> cultural norms that keep the worshipper from experiencing
> the reality of Christ. The norms that some want to escape are
> what they consider anachronistic traditions that have deadened
> church culture. The norms that others want to escape are the
> secular consumer values that they think have invaded church
> culture.[9]

In other words, there have been essentially two different
contemporary movements, one rejecting traditional forms
and the other seeking to recapture and renew them! The

---

9. B. Chapell, *Christ-Centered Worship: Letting the Gospel Shape Our
   Practice* (Grand Rapids: Baker Academic, 2009), p. 69.

positive reasons for these movements are amplified, as Chapell evaluates and critiques both 'Praise Worship Movements' and the 'Contemporary Classical Movement'.[10]

It is clearly important for Christians moving in apparently opposite directions to be aware of what motivates those with whom they disagree. It is also important to be more self-aware and self-critical while listening to the concerns of others. Both movements need to learn from each other, rather than being self-assured and dismissive of alternatives.[11]

Chapell highlights similarities between a number of historic, liturgical traditions and gives the impression that there really is only one 'gospel structure'. The structure he commends is essentially *adoration, confession, assurance, thanksgiving, petition, instruction, charge and blessing* (preceded by Holy Communion when appropriate). As well as being a liturgical sequence, Chappell says this describes 'the progress of the gospel in the life of an individual'.[12]

But does he read too much continuity and common cause into the pattern of liturgies he observes? Is this sequence the

---

10. However, see n. 4 above for a more complex assessment of the situation by L. Ruth, 'Rose by Any Other Name', pp. 33–51.

11. Chapell, *Christ-Centered Worship*, offers a more incisive criticism of the 'Praise Worship' tradition than the 'Contemporary Classical' trend. Some contemporary liturgical renewal has encouraged a more Catholic theology, especially concerning the Lord's Supper.

12. Ibid., p. 99. Chapell argues that the same sequence can be observed in the experience of the prophet in Isa. 6 and in the corporate pattern of worship highlighted in Deut. 5 and 2 Chr. 5 – 7. He rightly notes that we cannot 'press the details too tightly into our own liturgical pattern' (p. 106), but gives the impression that there is an Old Testament precedent for the sequence he has previously outlined. He goes on to draw New Testament parallels.

only way to convey the gospel story in liturgy? Does the gospel always progress in the life of an individual like this?

Different gospel-shaped services

Chapell outlines a theologically rich and pastorally helpful pattern of corporate worship that can be defended from Scripture and church history. But in the challenging environment of many alternatives today I want to ask whether this is the only way. Why not work from some other New Testament passages in which the gospel is differently expressed and various patterns of response are outlined and make these the basis for a variety of gospel-shaped services?

Chappell's approach reflects something of the sequence in Romans 3:9 – 4:12. A service based on this passage could involve the following:

> - Reflection on the nature of sin and its consequences, leading to a corporate expression of repentance (3:9–20)
> - Celebration of the grace of God in redeeming us through Christ with Bible readings and songs (3:21–26)
> - Teaching about justification by faith and its consequences, with the opportunity to respond in prayer and praise (3:27 – 4:12)

But Hebrews 10:11–25 might suggest a different pattern of service:

> - Celebration of the victory of Christ through his death, resurrection and ascension with Bible readings and songs (vv. 11–14)

- Teaching about the fulfilment of the promises of the New Covenant for us in Christ (vv. 15–18)
- Responding to the achievement of Christ by drawing near to God with repentance and faith (vv. 19–22), confessing and maintaining our hope together (v. 23), and spurring one another on toward love and good deeds by testimony, prayer and mutual exhortation (vv. 24–25)

1 John 1:1 – 2:11 might suggest another pattern of service:

- Celebration of the incarnation of the Son of God with Bible readings and songs (1:1–4)
- Challenge to confess sins and walk in the light, with the assurance of forgiveness and cleansing through Christ (1:5 – 2:2)
- Teaching about the practical implications of walking in the light, with an opportunity to respond with mutual exhortation, prayer and song (2:3–11)

Chapell rightly suggests that we should view corporate worship as 'nothing more, and nothing less, than a re-presentation of the gospel in the presence of God and his people for his glory and their good'.[13] But the New Testament presents the gospel in different ways to inform and challenge Christians in different contexts. Different passages could influence a range of service patterns, taking us on different spiritual and emotional journeys. In this way we

---

13. Ibid., p. 120.

could experience both familiarity and variety in our weekly gatherings.

> *Application question*: Does your pattern of service regularly present a gospel sequence, enabling the participants to respond to the richness of biblical revelation in ways that truly enable them to engage with God?

Ministering to one another as the New Testament directs

In chapter 3 we considered how the exercise of gifts and ministries in a congregational context contributes to the edification of the church. In the present chapter we noted how Hebrews 3:12–13 and 10:24–25 highlight the value of mutual encouragement or exhortation. This is often experienced in one-to-one relationships and small-group ministries, but in larger congregational gatherings the reading and exposition of Scripture is the major way in which it occurs.

Different contributions

Charismatic churches often provide more space for contributions from individuals in meetings, though these are not necessarily linked to the teaching time. More traditional churches may provide for congregational involvement in discussion, testimony and prayer, following the teaching and application of the Bible. In my view this is an aspect of what the New Testament means by prophesying in the broadest sense.

As proclaimed by Peter in Acts 2:14–21, 38–39, the prediction of Joel 2:28–32 has been fulfilled for everyone who calls on the name of the Lord Jesus for salvation. Those who have received the gift of the Holy Spirit can share their knowledge of the Lord and his grace in ways that help to strengthen and grow the church (see Acts 9:31).[14]

Individuals can contribute to the edification of the church in many ways: reading the Bible, preaching and teaching, giving a word of exhortation or testimony, leading in prayer, sharing in the music ministry, welcoming people, contributing financially, serving the practical needs of the congregation in management, audio-visual supervision, visitation of the sick and care for the needy (see Rom. 12:4–8). But how should contributions be organized and led when the church gathers?

Leadership of the gathering

The New Testament gives little indication of how early Christian gatherings were led. Acts records that the apostles took the initiative on certain occasions in the Jerusalem church (4:23–31; 6:2–6), though the heads of houses probably led meetings in homes (2:46–47). Some form of self-regulation in the exercise of gifts and ministries seems to have been Paul's desire in 1 Corinthians 14, where he gives guidelines about how to edify the church, but does not address the leaders about this.

Mostly, the New Testament indicates that leadership of congregations took place through teaching and exhortation (e.g. Acts 20:28–32; Gal. 6:6; Eph. 4:11–12; 1 Thess. 5:12–13; 1 – 2 Timothy; Titus). Prayer is highlighted as a significant aspect of such leadership in Acts 6:4. Praying with individuals must have been part of their ministry, as well as praying on their own, but Acts mostly gives examples of leaders praying

---

14. See D. G. Peterson, 'Prophetic Preaching in the Book of Acts', in P. A. Barker, R. J. Condie and A. S. Malone (eds.), *Serving God's Words: Windows on Preaching and Ministry* (Nottingham: Inter-Varsity Press, 2011), pp. 53–74 (esp. pp. 73–74).

when the church gathered (6:6; cf. 1:24–25; 4:24–31; 14:23).[15] Indeed, the combination of preaching and prayer has long been recognized as a significant way of pastoring Christ's flock.

The Protestant Reformers in the sixteenth century strongly objected to the sacrificial role that had been given to church leaders over the course of time, especially in connection with the conduct of the Lord's Supper or Holy Communion. They sought to recover the biblical emphasis on congregational leadership through preaching and prayer. Consequently, the liturgies they produced tended to limit the leadership of corporate worship to those who were ordained to preach.

In the twentieth century a concern emerged to recover the New Testament pattern of various people contributing to the edification of the church. This brought changes to the way services were conceived and conducted across the denominations. Greater informality and flexibility have accompanied changes of structure and content. More congregational members are now involved in the preparation and leadership of services. Spontaneous contributions are encouraged in different ways.

However, in reacting against a narrow view of leadership in corporate worship, some churches have moved to the point where the pastoral team is almost exclusively concerned with preaching, leaving the music team to plan and lead the singing, while those on different rosters read the Bible, lead in prayer and make other contributions.

---

15. Although Acts 4:24–31 records that many 'raised their voices together in prayer to God', it seems clear from what follows that one person led them in praise and petition. The prayer life of the earliest Christians is mentioned elsewhere in Acts: 1:14; 2:42, 46–47; 12:5; 13:2–3.

If those who lead never come together to reflect on what they are doing, to give feedback to one another, to pray and to co-ordinate their activities, the result can be disappointing. The sort of flow and direction in the service I have commended may not be there. Important elements may be left out and undue emphasis given to certain aspects of the gathering. Church leaders need to give regular instruction about the purpose of the gathering and how it should be structured and led. They should also model good leadership by regularly contributing in ways other than preaching.

The practice of making song leaders or music directors 'worship leaders' is unhelpful for several reasons.[16] First, it implies that worship is simply to be identified with praise, rather than being an aspect of the whole gathering and the agenda for everyday living. Secondly, it removes the congregational leader from the vital pastoral responsibility of overseeing and co-ordinating what is said and done when the church gathers. Thirdly, it hands over the planning and conduct of services to people who may be theologically immature and uninstructed.

Congregational leaders ought to reclaim the title of 'worship leaders' for themselves. They should teach that the preaching of God's word is what enables God's people to worship him acceptably, when they gather and when they disperse. But leaders should also consider how biblical teaching is expressed at every stage of the gathering and take time to instruct and equip those who contribute in various

---

16. B. Kauflin, *Worship Matters: Leading Others to Encounter the Greatness of God* (Wheaton: Crossway, 2008), pp. 21–26, 57–60, helpfully outlines how to be a faithful 'worship leader'. However, despite his argument on pp. 53–55, I think this term is best applied to congregational leaders, not to song leaders or musical directors.

ways to the edification of the church. All this is involved in effective pastoral leadership.

> *Application questions*: How adequately does your pattern of service involve people in ministry to one another and enable them to relate to God together? How does the leadership of gatherings function?

Summary

Every church has a regular pattern of service or liturgy, though this may be little more than a programme of apparently disconnected items. The challenge is to rethink what we are doing in the light of biblical teaching about what glorifies God and matures and encourages Christians in their discipleship. Put another way, how does the teaching about worship and edification in the preceding chapters apply to the planning and conduct of our church services, enabling us to encounter God and be encouraged in his service?

These issues are complex and suggest the need for theological and pastoral insight. Much can be gained from reflecting also on Christian practice through the centuries and evaluating what we do in the cultural context in which God has placed us. Just because a certain pattern of service has worked in one place will not mean that it is the best option for another.

Congregational leaders should see that the planning and conduct of church services is ultimately their responsibility. It is a ministry that ideally will dovetail with preaching. Of course, the New Testament encourages the sharing of gifts and ministries by others. So pastors should teach about the nature and purpose of the gathering and model how to make edifying contributions themselves. They should supervise the

process of planning and conducting edifying gatherings, even
if others are given substantial responsibility in this area. What
we do together should reflect the character of God in his
relationship with us (1 Cor. 14:33).

Questions for review and reflection

1. Why does the order and flow of a church service really
   matter?
2. How adequately do the 'three critical questions' enable
   us to explore and critique what we do when we gather
   together as Christ's people?
3. List ways in which biblical texts and biblical teaching
   might be heard in a Christian gathering.
4. What can we learn from the history of Christian
   liturgies or service patterns that might be helpful
   in congregational life today?

5. LISTENING TO GOD

We have already considered the importance of reading significant portions of the Bible aloud when the church gathers. We have also noted the ministry of exhortation that believers can have to one another in small groups or in the meeting of the whole church. When this prophetic-type ministry involves reflection on the meaning and application of Scripture, God's Spirit may address his people and challenge them in fresh ways. Now we focus on the place of preaching in the gathering and its significance for the life and health of the church.

When Cornelius the God-fearing Roman centurion finally met Peter the Jewish apostle, he declared, 'we are all here in the presence of God to listen to everything the Lord has commanded you to tell us' (Acts 10:33). God had brought them together in a remarkable way and so Cornelius expected God to speak to him through Peter's message. His expectation challenges many contemporary attitudes to congregational preaching.

Preaching revisited

Some consider preaching an ineffective and inadequate form of communication, no longer worthy of a central place in our gatherings. Perhaps they have heard too many long-winded, repetitive messages that were poorly delivered! There are exciting new means of teaching Christian truth, raising questions about the traditional form of pastoral exhortation, designed to stir people to some action or pattern of behaviour.

John Stott highlights three main arguments that have been used against preaching in the contemporary scene and responds to each one. He first identifies the anti-authority mood prevalent in Western culture that causes many to view the pulpit as 'a symbol of what they are rebelling against'.[1] Christians wishing to make an impact on such a culture can be deceived into thinking that only dialogue and more 'cool' forms of communication will get through to people.

Secondly, Stott begins to explore the way the cybernetics revolution has transformed our world. Since he wrote in 1982, amazing advances have taken place with the development of the Internet, satellite technology and mobile phones. These inventions have made it possible for information to spread across the world instantly and for individuals to be caught up in dramas and debates in faraway places. Christians have begun to exploit the potential for evangelism, apologetics, teaching, the sharing of music, and electronic books. Many churches now use video projection for songs, Bible passages, sermon outlines, video clips and input from someone outside the local context.

---

1. J. R. W. Stott, *I Believe in Preaching* (London: Hodder & Stoughton, 1982); *Between Two Worlds: The Art of Preaching in the Twentieth Century* (Grand Rapids: Eerdmans, 1982), p. 52.

Stott focuses on the impact of television on preaching, which 'makes it harder for people to listen attentively and responsively, and therefore for preachers to hold a congregation's attention, let alone secure an appropriate response'.[2] We could also consider the effect of other electronic media on what we do together. For example, when we address God by reading words together from a screen, does it change the character of prayer? What is the impact of using video clips, visual art or music in a sermon? What is the value of having someone address a congregation through a video link?

Preachers and service leaders need to reckon with ministry in a media-saturated society and be discerning about the positive and negative implications for their gatherings. Nevertheless, Stott argues that a biblical view of preaching suggests a unique form of communication, 'for here are God's people assembled in God's presence to hear God's word from God's minister'.[3] The preacher's role in this process will be explored below.

Finally, Stott argues that 'the contemporary loss of confidence in the gospel is the most basic of all hindrances to preaching'.[4] Doubt about the relevance and divine authority of the Bible is widespread. The centrality of the gospel to the Bible's message is not grasped and its power to change lives is not appreciated. Alternative patterns of Christian influence in the world are sought.

Even Bible-believing churches can favour singing or other ministries to such an extent that the Scriptures are hardly ever read or expounded. What is read may be only loosely

---

2. Ibid., p. 70.

3. Ibid., p. 82.

4. Ibid., p. 83. See R. A. Mohler, *He Is Not Silent: Preaching in a Postmodern World* (Chicago: Moody, 2008).

connected with the sermon, which may be very experientially oriented and be only superficially biblical. The focus may be on encountering God in the prayers and praises of his people or in sharing the Lord's Supper, rather than through the preaching of God's word.

Pastors need to be convinced that God speaks when the Bible is faithfully taught. They also need to help their people understand how God confronts us through the event of preaching, despite the inadequacies of the preacher! Those who prepare for and lead Christian gatherings need to reflect on the way this expectation might be expressed in the pattern and content of services.

Gospel and Scripture

The earliest Christians in Jerusalem 'devoted themselves to the apostles' teaching and to fellowship, to the breaking of bread and to prayer' (Acts 2:42). Day after day they assembled in the temple courts to hear the apostles teach from the Scriptures and proclaim the gospel (2:46; 4:1–4; 5:42). As the believing community grew, others were appointed to care for the needy in their midst, so that the apostles could give their full attention to prayer and 'the ministry of the word' (6:1–6).

Ministry of the word

Since 'the word' in Acts normally refers to the gospel, this expression shows that their teaching ministry consistently had a gospel focus.[5] A variety of other preachers soon began to share in this ministry, doubtless inspired by the example and teaching of the apostles. They proclaimed Christ to indi-

---

5. See D. G. Peterson, *The Acts of the Apostles*, PNTC (Grand Rapids: Eerdmans; Nottingham: Apollos, 2009), pp. 32–36, 70–71.

viduals and households outside Jerusalem (8:26–40; 10:34–48), and planted churches wherever they went (8:4–13; 11:19–26).

Evangelism and the nurture of believers through teaching continued in the missionary journeys of Paul. Sometimes he taught in synagogues (13:14–48; 17:1–12; 19:8), sometimes in more public places (16:13–34; 19:9–10) and sometimes in homes (18:7–8; 20:7–12, 20; 28:16–31). Although the pattern of evangelism was different where audiences were unfamiliar with the Jewish Scriptures (14:15–18; 17:22–31), Paul's ultimate aim was to proclaim 'Jesus and the resurrection' to Jews and Gentiles whenever he could (17:18; 22:2–21; 23:6; 24:10–21; 26:2–29; 28:20).

Acts indicates a strong connection between evangelism, the defence of Christianity against misunderstanding, and the nurture of believers. The earliest Christians gathered to hear gifted teachers explain from the Scriptures how Jesus is Lord and Christ and how the salvation promised in the Scriptures was achieved through his death, resurrection and ascension. Almost all of the recorded speeches present different ways of doing this. Even Paul's address to pagans in Athens teaches biblical theology, without quoting specific verses, and seeks to turn unbelievers to Christ (17:22–31).[6]

The earliest Christian believers were taught by those whom God sent to proclaim Christ from the Old Testament and deal with objections to their message. The apostles had spent time listening to Jesus explain how the Scriptures would be fulfilled (Luke 24:44–49) and they followed his pattern in teaching

---

6. See ibid., pp. 493–503.

> others. 'Pastors and teachers' were then raised up and used by the ascended Lord, together with apostles, prophets and evangelists, to 'equip his people for works of service, so that the body of Christ may be built up' (Eph. 4:11–12).[7]

Pastoring through teaching

Although most of the teaching in Acts is to mixed audiences, there must have been times when the focus was simply on believers, where questions were asked and answered, the Scriptures were applied to pastoral issues and the churches were strengthened (11:26; 20:2, 7–12).

Only one speech in Acts is specifically directed to believers. The context is not a gathering of the whole church but a meeting of elders or overseers (20:18–35). Paul reviews the nature of his extensive ministry in Ephesus and describes it as preaching 'anything that would be helpful to you' (v. 20). His aim was to declare to both Jews and Greeks 'that they must turn to God in repentance and have faith in our Lord Jesus' (v. 21). To achieve this end, he testified to 'the good news of God's grace' (v. 24). More broadly, he preached the 'kingdom' of God (v. 25), which appears to be the same thing as proclaiming 'the whole will of God' (v. 27). Paul preached Christ by explaining from the Scriptures how God's kingdom plan and purpose had been fulfilled for Jews and Gentiles (see 13:16–48; 17:2–3).

As well as challenging unbelievers in this way, Paul taught Christians to understand the gospel more and more in the

---

7. P. T. O'Brien, *The Letter to the Ephesians*, PNTC (Grand Rapids: Eerdmans; Leicester: Apollos, 1999), p. 300, argues that the terms 'pastor' and 'teacher' describe overlapping functions, but distinct ministries: 'all pastors teach (since teaching is an essential part of pastoral ministry), but not all teachers are also pastors'.

light of Old Testament expectations. Moreover, for three years he did not stop warning the Ephesian elders about the danger of false teaching arising from their midst and dividing the church (Acts 20:29–31). As he departed, he committed those leaders 'to God and to the word of his grace, which can build you up and give you an inheritance among all those who are sanctified' (v. 32).

'The word of his grace' in this context refers to the gospel proclamation of the benefits of Christ's atoning death, by which he 'bought' the church (v. 28), and his resurrection, by which he enabled his sanctified people to share together in his promised eternal inheritance (v. 32). Even these brief allusions show how Paul's gospel presentation was influenced by Old Testament theology and expectations. This biblical gospel forms, matures and sustains the church as the people of God. It is also the antidote to false teaching and division amongst Christians.

What can we learn from this brief survey of Acts that is applicable to our contemporary scene? Here are four suggestions.

- Trust that God's Spirit continues to speak through the reading and exposition of inspired Scripture, illuminating and applying it to human hearts according to his sovereign will (see 2 Tim. 3:14–17; 2 Pet. 1:19–21).
- Understand that the gospel is the ultimate word of God that needs to be heard in various ways by unbelievers, so that they may be saved, and by believers, so that they may be matured and sustained in Christ (see 2 Tim. 4:1–8).

- Discover how the gospel is still the key to explaining and applying the Scriptures faithfully (see Luke 24:44–49).[8]
- Be convinced that, although effective communication involves teaching and exhortation, the element of proclamation is critical, because the preacher is declaring what God has revealed about his character, will and accomplishments (see Col. 1:28).

Proclamation, teaching and exhortation

Not every sermon that claims to be biblical is worthy of that description. For example, biblical texts can be used as 'pegs' on which preachers hang their 'hats'. A sermon may be about some moral or social issue that really has nothing to do with a biblical passage. It may involve pious spiritual lessons that come from the experience of the preacher, rather than from Scripture, or it may seem like a lecture in theology!

Genuinely biblical preaching will expose the message of a biblical text or some segment of the Bible's teaching and let it speak to the situation of the hearers. John Stott describes it as a bridge between the world of the text and the world of the listeners. The task of preachers 'is to enable God's revealed truth to flow out of the Scriptures into the lives of men and women of today'.[9] Haddon Robinson identifies the critical role of the preacher in the process:

---

8. G. Goldsworthy, *Preaching the Whole Bible as Christian Scripture: The Application of Biblical Theology to Expository Preaching* (Leicester: Inter-Varsity Press, 2000), is a helpful guide in this connection. But a study of the sermons in Acts would also be a good starting point.

9. Stott, *Preaching*, p. 138.

> Expository preaching is the communication of a biblical concept, derived from and transmitted through a historical, grammatical and literary study of a passage in its context, which the Holy Spirit first applies to the personality and experience of the preacher, then through the preacher, applies to the hearers.[10]

Preachers must work hard at understanding and applying the text, first to themselves and then to the congregation. But that does not simply mean thinking up clever illustrations. Relevant preaching occurs when the unique message of the Bible intersects the unique situation of the people addressed. A good preacher will get to know the aspirations and fears of the congregation, their questions and their doubts. When these are taken into account, the preacher effectively enters into a dialogue with the people when explaining and applying the Scriptures.

Heralding and teaching

What we call 'preaching' today may include three different, but related, New Testament activities: proclamation, teaching, and exhortation. The Greek word most commonly translated 'preach' always carried the basic meaning 'cry aloud', 'proclaim', 'declare' or 'announce'. In modern terms we could perhaps identify this activity with advertising. A related term is the verb 'evangelize', which conveys the sense of announcing news.

Jesus appeared as a herald of the kingdom of God, offering salvation through his preaching to those who responded with repentance and faith (e.g. Mark 1:14–15; Luke 4:21; 7:22). His preaching occurred in the synagogues (e.g. Mark 1:39; Luke

---

10. H. W. Robinson, *Biblical Preaching: The Development and Delivery of Expository Messages*, 2nd ed. (Grand Rapids: Baker, 1993), p. 21.

4:44) and more publicly in the towns and open spaces (e.g. Mark 5:20; Matt. 11:1). As part of his preaching or heralding activity he used an amazing array of teaching techniques such as parables, wisdom sayings, proverbs and questioning.

> Teaching is not always preaching in the sense of proclamation. It may involve systematic exposition of a passage of Scripture or engagement with a theological or ethical issue. But preaching in the sense of proclaiming the gospel will normally involve teaching of some kind. Although contemporary preachers ought to use a variety of teaching methods appropriate to the occasion and subject matter, the aim of gospel proclamation is to challenge people to respond to and receive what God offers us in Christ.

The sermons in Acts show that teaching about the way Scripture has been fulfilled was an important part of the apostolic proclamation about Jesus and the achievement of God's kingdom plan. The New Testament epistles reveal the sort of ethical and doctrinal teaching that was also part of the communication process when churches were founded (e.g. 1 Thess. 4:1–10; 5:1–11; 1 Cor. 11:2, 23–26).

Early Christian preaching involved proving certain matters (Acts 9:22), disputing with opponents (9:29) and reasoning from the Scriptures (17:2–3). Nevertheless, the task of heralding what God has done in Christ was fundamental to the activity.

Exhortation and warning

The third dimension to the process of Christian communication is often conveyed by the use of terms such as 'exhort', 'encourage' or 'warn' in the New Testament. For example,

Paul's command to Timothy was literally 'devote yourself to the public reading of Scripture, to *exhortation* and to teaching' (1 Tim. 4:13). People need to be persuaded about the urgency, the relevance and the truth of the message. But if persuasive techniques are used, the motives and methods of the preacher must be honest and sincere (1 Thess. 2:3).

Paul puts together these three aspects of Christian communication, when he describes his own ministry in this way: '[Christ] is the one we proclaim, admonishing and teaching everyone with all wisdom, so that we may present everyone fully mature in Christ' (Col. 1:28).

Different types of biblical preaching
Topical preaching
This involves examining a theological theme or an ethical issue, usually employing a collection of biblical texts from different contexts. Since it deals directly with matters of concern to the congregation or tackles current problems in the community, it can be quite popular.

There is a danger, however, in using the Bible selectively, taking verses out of context and not letting the Bible provide all the answers we need to hear on the topic. There is also the danger of confusing the congregation by using too many texts from too many contexts. These difficulties can be overcome by careful selection and exposition of a number of key texts over several weeks, contributing to a series of sermons on the subject.

Textual preaching
This involves the explanation and application of one or two verses in a sequence. It gives an opportunity for in-depth treatment of important doctrines or themes in a memorable way. Not too much biblical material is given for people

to assimilate in one sermon and the text is carefully and faithfully mined for its treasures. This is a good way to introduce biblical preaching and show people how to interpret texts. But the potential dangers of this method must also be noted.

Textual preaching can easily isolate verses from their literary and theological context. Preachers, by using inappropriate methods, can actually set a bad example. Again, there is the danger of not letting the Bible set the agenda for our preaching. We use it to answer *our* questions but will not let it ask us *its* questions. Textual preachers tend to come back to their favourites regularly and sometimes use these verses to expound their own pet theories. Finally, there is the problem of not giving people a broad enough knowledge of the Bible or of whole sections of the Bible.

Systematic exposition of biblical passages

This method potentially overcomes a number of the difficulties noted above. As the sermons move progressively through a biblical book, Scripture itself sets the agenda and confronts us with its own questions. It forces us to look at topics and perspectives on topics we might not otherwise consider. Bible study groups can be helpfully integrated with a programme of systematic expository preaching. The participants can be encouraged to work hard at the application and implementation of the teaching given in sermons.[11]

---

11. Many insights about biblical preaching can be found in H. W. Robinson and C. B. Larson (eds.), *The Art and Craft of Biblical Preaching: A Comprehensive Resource for Today's Communicators* (Grand Rapids: Zondervan, 2005), and P. A. Barker, R. J. Condie and S. Malone, *Serving God's Words: Windows on Preaching and Ministry* (Nottingham: Inter-Varsity Press, 2011).

> This method offers *a built-in variety*, which is good for the preacher and good for the congregation. Preachers are forced to engage in serious Bible study as part of their preparation and are delivered from the uncertainty of knowing which text to choose each week. Congregations are taught how to handle the Bible for themselves and their general knowledge of Scripture and its themes is gradually built up. There is less chance of verses being expounded out of context. Each week in a series brings a clearer understanding of the message of the book being studied.

Once again, however, there are dangers to be avoided. There is always the temptation to try to handle too much Scripture in one sermon. This may mean that there is only time to explain the text and not apply it. It can also mean becoming too slick and superficial in handling the passage. There are certainly occasions for preaching on large slabs of Scripture, but different methods of presentation may be required, so that the congregation is not inflicted with spiritual indigestion.[12]

Expository sermons can become too predictable and heavy, sounding more like a lecture than a sermon. The preacher needs to prepare the exegesis or interpretation of the passage early in the week and allow plenty of time to consider the best way to apply the message and persuade the congregation to respond. Different ways of expounding a passage need to be tried, such as the use of key verses to open up the meaning of a passage or using one verse as a window into the whole passage.

---

12. Robinson, *Biblical Preaching*, pp. 33–46, writes about the need for a sermon to convey one major idea, which is the theme of the portion of Scripture on which it is based.

Preaching for too long on a particular section of Scripture can also lead to a feeling of boredom on the part of the congregation, unless the preacher is extremely skilled. Variety can be achieved by breaking up a series with a focus on some other part of Scripture or by having a series of topical sermons. Variety also comes from planning a proper preaching programme for the year, with adequate attention to Old and New Testaments and the various elements within them (history, prophecy, wisdom, gospel, epistle).[13]

Summary

There are many ways of communicating the message of the Bible and helping people understand its relevance, especially using the electronic resources available to us today. But it is clear from the example of Jesus and the teaching of the apostles that preaching or proclamation is especially suited to conveying divine revelation and challenging people to respond appropriately.

The gospel is a key to explaining the Scriptures and applying the message to unbelievers and believers alike faithfully. The gospel in its many facets and expressions should therefore be a key aspect of Christian preaching. According to the topic and the occasion, supportive argument, defence and appeals to respond appropriately will also be involved in varying measures.

Christians need to be assured that, when the Bible is read and expounded with the direction and enabling of the Holy Spirit, God's voice is heard. As when Peter met Cornelius, preaching can be a prophetic activity, confronting the hearers

---

13. J. Arthurs, *Preaching with Variety: How to Recreate the Dynamics of Biblical Genres* (Grand Rapids: Kregel, 2007), suggests different ways of preaching on the different types of literature found in the Bible.

with God's character and will so that their lives are transformed. As with Paul's sermon to the Ephesian elders, preaching can be a pastoral activity, reminding God's people of his grace towards them and challenging them collectively to faithfulness and obedience.

The challenge for preachers is to consider whether they give enough attention to the reading and exposition of Scripture. They should also consider the sort of response to the ministry of the word they encourage and reflect on how this is expressed in the gathering. How much time is given to the preparation of every aspect of this ministry?

Questions for review and reflection

1. What are some of the difficulties people in your church express about preaching? How could these be overcome?
2. To what extent is the systematic reading aloud of Scripture part of your congregational tradition? What hinders this activity?
3. How can preaching be a pastoral ministry?
4. What did you learn from this brief exploration of preaching in the New Testament?

6. PRAYING TOGETHER

Prayer is foundational to the Christian life from start to finish. A genuine relationship with God begins when we call upon him in the name of Jesus to forgive our sins and give us his Spirit (Acts 2:38). 'The Spirit of Christ' (Rom. 8:9) enables us to relate to God as Father and engage in trusting, persistent prayer just as Jesus did.[1] When we cry 'Abba, Father', the Spirit of God's Son testifies with our own spirit that we are truly God's children (Rom. 8:15–16; cf. Gal. 4:6–7). This uniquely Christian way of addressing God is his gift to those who receive 'adoption to sonship' by turning to Christ as Saviour and Lord (Gal. 4:4–5).[2]

---

1. Luke's Gospel particularly shows Jesus at prayer in a range of circumstances (3:21; 4:42; 6:12; 9:18; 10:21; 11:1; 22:39–44; 23:46).

2. Addressing God with the Aramaic *Abba* was an indication of Jesus' unique relationship with the Father. When we receive the Spirit who brings about our adoption to sonship, we are invited to address God with similar intimacy. Men and women together share in this new status and privilege (see Gal. 3:28).

Those who know Jesus as the exalted Son of God and heavenly high priest continue to approach God through him, asking confidently for mercy and grace to live faithfully as his children (Heb. 4:14–16). Biblically shaped prayer does not simply ask God to meet our material needs, but begs him to sustain and mature us as disciples of Christ (Eph. 3:14–19; Col. 1:9–14; 1 Thess. 3:12–13). Spirit-directed prayer seeks wisdom from God so that we may fulfil his purpose for us and be fruitful in his service (Jas 1:4–8). Such prayer should characterize our individual lives and our gatherings as his people.

Learning from the Lord's Prayer

When Jesus taught his disciples how to pray, he first expressed a passion for God's name to be hallowed, for his kingdom to come and his will to be done. Then he invited them to ask for daily sustenance, for forgiveness, for resistance to temptation and deliverance from evil (Matt. 6:9–13; cf. Luke 11:1–4). Although some regard the Lord's Prayer as simply a pattern or guide for us to follow, it would seem from Luke 11:2 that Jesus gave the prayer as an actual form of words for disciples to use ('When you pray, say . . . ').

Apart from its actual use, it is worth asking whether our gatherings truly reflect what Jesus taught in this prayer. For example, is praise and thanksgiving offered to proclaim the character of God and honour his name or is it designed to create a mood and prepare for something else? Do the words we sing really matter or is the music considered more important? Do we merely sing at particular points in our gatherings because that is what we have always done?

Is there a kingdom focus to our prayers and praises? Do they reflect 'the whole will of God' (Acts 20:27), so that believers understand and seek to serve God's purpose for his world? Does the pattern of our prayer together help us acknowledge our sins and seek God's forgiveness? Do our prayers give us a sense of urgency about resisting temptation and seeking deliverance from evil?

In many churches I have visited 'the prayer time' is a discrete moment when petitions are offered for the sick and the needy, for the work of the gospel, and perhaps also for those in authority (see 1 Tim. 2:1–6). But there may be little prayer before or after this moment, because so many other things are on the agenda. Very few service leaders seem to understand that prayer should be the cement holding together the different things we do together and giving a Godward focus to every aspect of the gathering.

Meditation on the Lord's Prayer might be a good starting point for reconsidering the structure and contents of our gatherings. Jesus teaches a way of approaching God that puts his concerns before our own. He invites us to be specific about our material and spiritual needs, but within the context of seeking first 'his kingdom and his righteousness' (Matt. 6:33). This pattern is also found in other New Testament contexts, as believers pray together (e.g. Acts 4:23–30), or as Paul reports his own pattern of thanksgiving and prayer (e.g. Phil. 1:3–11; Col. 1:3–14), presumably to encourage his readers to imitate it in their personal and corporate lives.

> A gathering reflecting the pattern of the Lord's Prayer might begin with songs of praise about the character and deeds of God ('Our Father in heaven, hallowed be your name'). This might be followed by prayer for God's kingdom plan to impact our lives more decisively and for God to advance his work in the world ('your kingdom come, your will be done on earth as it is in heaven'). Prayer for God to provide for our needs could lead to a time of reading and reflecting on the Scriptures ('Give

us today our daily bread'). This might be followed by a confession of sin, seeking his forgiveness, and a prayer for more faithful discipleship ('forgive us our debts, as we also have forgiven our debtors. And lead us not into temptation, but deliver us from evil'). The conclusion to the service could be doxology and praise ('for yours is the kingdom and the power and the glory for ever. Amen.').[3]

Relating to God and to one another

Prayer is essential for a fruitful and lasting relationship with God through the Lord Jesus Christ. By this means he enables us to stand firm against sin, seek his guidance, make wise decisions, submit to his will and serve him in specific ways. Prayer is the means by which we continue to express our trust in God, maintain our dependence upon him in all circumstances, and experience his grace in everyday contexts. Prayer is an essential means of engaging with God together. But the apostle Paul also points to the 'horizontal' or interpersonal benefit of praying together.

Praying together

Writing about the edification of the church, Paul tells the Corinthians:

> I will pray with my spirit, but I will also pray with my understanding; I will sing with my spirit, but I will also sing

---

3. The praise conclusion to the Lord's Prayer appears only in some later manuscripts of Matthew's Gospel. It is recorded in a footnote in most translations. However, this doxology reflects the sentiments expressed in the first few lines of the Lord's Prayer and has been viewed by Christians as a fitting conclusion to the prayer from the earliest centuries.

with my understanding. Otherwise when you are praising God in the Spirit, how can someone else, who is now put in the position of an enquirer, say 'Amen' to your thanksgiving, since they do not know what you are saying? You are giving thanks well enough, but no one else is edified. (1 Cor. 14:15–17)

Public prayer, praise and thanksgiving should be offered to God in a way that benefits other believers.[4] Praying in tongues without interpretation or praying in a way that inhibits others from joining in hinders Christian fellowship. Such prayer is not honouring to God because it puts others in the position of an outsider or 'enquirer', not feeling that they belong. Singing is also meant to be a way of expressing ourselves towards God while edifying the church (Col. 3:16–17; Eph. 5:18–20). We shall consider what the Bible teaches about singing together in chapter 8.

Significantly, Paul expected Gentile Christians to use the Hebrew word *'āmēn* as a response to the prayers and praises of others (1 Cor. 14:16). It is a way of agreeing with what has been said and therefore a way of being united with others in their approach to God. This congregational response is found in certain Old Testament contexts (e.g. 1 Chr. 16:36; Neh. 8:6; Pss 41:13; 72:19; 89:52), and finds its ultimate use in the heavenly worship portrayed in Revelation 5:13–14.

Prayers that are unbiblical in their content or that are superficial will contribute little to the edification of the church. Prayers that go on for too long without inviting a response

---

4. D. A. Carson, *A Call to Spiritual Reformation: Priorities from Paul and His Prayers* (Grand Rapids: Baker, 1992), p. 35, argues from the example of Jesus in John 11:41–42 that there is 'ample reason to reflect on just what my prayer, rightly directed to God, is saying to the people who hear me'.

will not hold the attention of the congregation. Prayers that 'preach' to people, rather than focusing their attention on God, will be annoying and unhelpful. Those who lead in prayer should make it easy for others to say 'Amen' or express their agreement in some other way.

> There are different Christian traditions regarding the saying of 'Amen'. Some churches invite a formal conclusion to prayers, perhaps preceding 'Amen' with words such as 'through Jesus Christ our Lord' or 'to him be glory for ever and ever'. In other churches people say 'Amen' informally throughout a prayer, even at the end of every sentence! In some churches there is barely a whisper of 'Amen' when prayer is finished. Clearly, some sort of corporate response is encouraged by the apostle. Another way of doing this is to conclude a prayer with a petition such as 'Lord in your mercy', to which the people respond 'hear our prayer' or something similar.

Spontaneous or prepared?

Spontaneous prayer can be meaningful and helpful. But writing some prayers in advance may edify the church more effectively because the content has been carefully considered. Alternatively, a leader may suggest a series of topics and invite others to respond spontaneously, providing also a previously prepared beginning and ending to the session or to each segment of prayer.

Some churches invite members of the congregation to join together in saying set prayers. Books of prayers can be a great resource, especially for praying on special occasions. If it seems unnatural, even unspiritual, to recite words written by someone else, it should be remembered that a number of biblical prayers, including the Lord's Prayer, appear to have been composed for corporate use (e.g. Pss 46, 67, 74, 76, 80). Christians throughout the ages have followed various biblical models when composing prayers for believers to say together or responsively.

Ralph Martin argues for a thoughtful combination of set prayers and free praying, when he says:

> Care needs to be taken to avoid the two extremes of an over-simplified 'nursery' praying which most will find embarrassing, and a convoluted or esoteric style of praying that leaves the people confused and threatened. Dignity need not be sacrificed at the expense of simplicity; and simplicity need not be reduced to the language of the kindergarten.[5]

In my experience a blend of set prayers with more spontaneous offerings works well. Simply repeating the same form of words together each week can be dreary and uninspiring. Alternatives need to be provided, maybe on a monthly cycle. But a service involving only spontaneous prayer can be shallow, repetitive and unspiritual in its own way.

Even a little preparation may enrich the total experience of praying together. Many Christians find it difficult to reflect the depths of biblical praying when asked to pray spontaneously in a gathering. Using some carefully crafted words in a written prayer can be encouraging to everyone involved. Reflecting on a biblical passage can be a great stimulus for meaningful prayer, turning its message into a series of petitions, perhaps also with praise and thanksgiving.

---

5. R. P. Martin, *The Worship of God: Some Theological, Pastoral, and Practical Reflections* (Grand Rapids: Eerdmans, 1982), p. 31. His evaluation of the strengths and weaknesses of set prayers and free praying is on pp. 38–41.

Biblical patterns of prayer

The critical issue with corporate prayer is the extent to which it reflects biblical teaching and biblical ways of approaching God. We have much to learn from the content and the patterns of prayer found throughout the Bible. There are many different situations in which God's people prayed and many different ways in which they expressed their confidence in God.[6]

Individual models

Abraham prayed with increasing boldness for the people of Sodom to be delivered from God's judgment (Gen. 18:22–32). Moses asked God not to punish the Israelites for their idolatry (Exod. 32:30–32). David prayed for his own sins to be forgiven and for God to create in him a pure heart (Ps. 51). Daniel prayed on behalf of his people in exile that God would restore them to their homeland (Dan. 9:4–19).

David taught the Israelites how to praise God for his faithfulness and cry out for his mercy (1 Chr. 16:7–36). When Solomon dedicated the temple, he taught the people how to approach God in prayer for everyday needs (2 Chr. 6:14–42). When Ezra read to the people from the Book of the Law, he led them in praise to God (Neh. 8:5–6). This encouraged the Israelites to confess their sins, to praise God for his many mercies, and to seek his deliverance from foreign oppression (Neh. 9:1–37).

---

6. E. P. Clowney, 'A Biblical Theology of Prayer', in D. A. Carson (ed.), *Teach Us to Pray: Prayer in the Bible and the World*, World Evangelical Fellowship (Grand Rapids: Baker; Exeter: Paternoster, 1990), pp. 136–173, provides an excellent reflection on the character and significance of prayer throughout the Bible.

Praying with the Psalms

The book of Psalms provides the most extensive resource of prayers and praises in the Bible. Some express the sense of being forsaken by God, followed by words of confidence about deliverance (e.g. 6, 13, 22, 38). Some simply praise God for who he is, and for his marvellous deeds (e.g. 9, 26, 40, 44, 65, 66). Some recite the history of God's saving actions (e.g. 78, 105, 106, 114, 136), while others invoke or rejoice in the judgment of God (e.g. 7, 9, 36, 50, 58, 67, 94, 96, 98, 137, 149).

'One of the ways we learn good communication habits with God is by participating in corporate worship.'[7] We have much to learn from the language and approach of the biblical psalms and from experiencing their use in the gathering of God's people.

It may not be easy to use every one of the psalms corporately, but some may provide an ideal response to readings from Scripture or to sermons about related themes. Very few contemporary songs deal with suffering, testing, loneliness, persecution or deliverance from sickness and death, as many psalms do. Some psalms point us particularly to the person and work of the Lord Jesus (e.g. 2, 22, 69, 110). With careful introduction, these may be used to affirm our trust in Christ together.

> Psalms or portions of psalms can be used at different points in a service. Some can be used as a call to worship or as an expression of praise at the beginning of a gathering (e.g. 95, 96, 98,

---

7. J. D. Witvliet, *The Biblical Psalms in Christian Worship: A Brief Introduction and Guide to Resources* (Grand Rapids: Eerdmans, 2007), p. 11. Witvliet, pp. 16–35, outlines seven lessons the Psalms teach us about prayer.

100). Some can be used as a challenge to listen carefully to the word of God and respond with obedient faith (e.g. 1, 15, 19, 119). Some express repentance and the need for forgiveness or moral transformation (e.g. 32, 51, 130, 139). Many express the need for confidence in God in the face of uncertainty, doubt and suffering, and would provide an ideal response to readings and teaching on those topics.

Prayer, praise and thanksgiving

The word 'prayer' is often used to describe any kind of communication with God. But it is important to note that in the New Testament all the prayer words mean 'asking'. Other terms are employed for giving thanks or praising God. The apostle Paul uses a number of the asking words, together with 'thanksgiving', when he encourages the Philippians not to be anxious about anything. 'In every situation,' he writes, 'by *prayer* and *petition*, with thanksgiving, present your *requests* to God' (Phil. 4:6).

Thanksgiving in Scripture is normally addressed directly to God (e.g. Ps. 118; Col. 1:3–4; Rev. 11:17–18). Praise may be either directed to God or given indirectly, as we sing and talk about the goodness and greatness of God to one another (e.g. Ps. 113; Rom. 11:33–36; Eph. 1:3–14). Like praise, thanksgiving is an important aspect of our corporate testimony to Christ and a means of mutual encouragement (1 Cor. 14:16; Phil. 4:4–6; Col. 1:11–12).

God brings glory to himself, as he works through the ministry he commands us to have to each other in prayer, praise and thanksgiving. By this means we can acknowledge what he has done for us in the past and express our confidence in what he has for us in the future. More will be said about this in the next chapter.

Reflecting on God and his will

Paul's letter to the Romans shows us how the apostle's life was filled with prayer and praise, even as he was writing! As he reflects on what God has said and done in creation and redemption and in the transforming work of the gospel, he invites his readers to join him in prayer, praise and thanksgiving.

1. A reported *thanksgiving*: Paul tells the Roman Christians how he thanks God that their faith is being reported all over the world (1:8).

2. A reported *petition*: Paul reveals how he has been praying for God to make it possible for him to visit them (1:9–10).

3. *Doxologies*: Paul identifies God as the one who should be glorified or praised for ever (1:25; 9:5; 11:33–36; 16:27).

4. *Thanksgivings*: Paul gives thanks to God for particular gospel blessings (6:17–18; 7:25).

5. *Specific teaching* about prayer and the Spirit (8:15–16, 26–27).

6. *Exhortations to prayer* (12:12, 14 [general]; 15:30–32 [specific]).

7. *Wish prayers*: indirect prayers, formally addressed to the readers, telling them what Paul asks God to do for them (1:7; 15:5–6, 13, 33; 16:20).

The development of prayer and praise in a congregational context should be encouraged by biblical teaching about the character of God and how he works through his people to achieve his purposes. Believers also need to be taught about the nature and extent of God-honouring prayer. Furthermore, they need to hear good examples of biblically informed prayer in church and be shown how to pray that way themselves. In particular, the biblical pattern of recollecting, confessing, praising and then asking for God's will to be done ought to be modelled.[8]

Praying for other believers

Paul regularly gives thanks for and reports how he prays for the churches to which he writes. Sometimes his petitions arise directly from his thanksgivings.[9] So, for example, in Colossians 1:5–6 Paul gives thanks for 'the faith and love that spring from the hope stored up for you in heaven and about which you have already heard in the true message of the gospel that has come to you'. He is grateful that the gospel is 'bearing fruit and grow-ing throughout the whole world', just as it has been growing in Colossae. Then, when he reports his prayers for them, he picks up and develops some of the same themes again:

> We continually ask God to fill you with the knowledge of his will . . . so that you may live a life worthy of the Lord and please him in every way: bearing fruit in every good work, growing in the knowledge of God, being strengthened with all power according to his glorious might so that you may have great endurance and patience, and giving joyful thanks to the Father, who has qualified you to share in the inheritance of his holy people in the kingdom of light. (Col. 1:9b–12)

---

8. See H. O. Old, *Leading in Prayer: A Workbook for Ministers* (Grand Rapids: Eerdmans, 1995); Calvin Institute of Christian Worship, *The Worship Source Book* (Grand Rapids: Baker, 2004); P. Law, *Praying with the Bible* (London: SPCK, 2007).

9. Carson, *Call to Spiritual Reformation*, p. 40, argues that 'thanksgiving is a fundamental component of the mental framework that largely controls Paul's intercession'. Paul looks for things in the lives of other Christians for which he can give thanks to God and makes such thanksgiving the basis for prayer.

Paul reports his thanksgiving and prayer in this way to introduce some of the concerns of his letter. But he also seeks to encourage the readers to follow his example when they pray for one another and for other believers.

To what extent do our corporate prayers reflect the sort of thanksgiving found in Paul's letters? Do they express his concern for a deeper knowledge of God's will, so that we may live a life worthy of the Lord and please him in every way?[10] How often do you hear people in church praying that we may bear fruit in every good work, grow in the knowledge of God, and be strengthened by him to endure with patience and joyful thanks?

Praying more broadly

As well as the things suggested for prayer by Jesus and by Paul in the opening paragraphs of some of his letters, we are encouraged by the New Testament to pray for the following:

- National and civic leaders (1 Tim. 2:1–4; cf. Rom. 13:1–7; 1 Pet. 2:13–17)
- Church leaders and missionary activity (Rom. 15:30–32; Eph. 6:18–20; Col. 4:2–4; Heb. 13:18–19)
- The sick (Jas 5:13–18; cf. 2 Cor. 12:8–9)
- Christians who go astray (1 John 5:16; cf. Jas 5:19–20)

Prayer bulletins detailing local needs and requests related to the work of the gospel or social and political concerns in

---

10. Carson, ibid., p. 101, notes that there is really only one petition in Col. 1:9–14 (that God might 'fill you with the knowledge of his will through all the wisdom and understanding that the Spirit gives'), followed by 'a statement of its purpose and a description of the way God's answer to the petition works out in daily life'.

the wider world can be an incentive for members of a church to pray.

Answers to prayer ought to feature prominently in our public meetings, by way of testimony or report, and in our church publications. Answers to prayer can be the basis for thanksgiving to God and an encouragement for his people to pray more boldly and persistently. Congregations need to know that God answers prayer and so glorify him accordingly.

Prayer may occur at several stages throughout a gathering:

- *At the beginning*, to approach God with penitence or to ask him to minister to the congregation in some way
- *Linked with songs*, to express more fully a hope or desire suggested by a song
- *Before the reading and teaching of the Bible*, to ask for attention, understanding and an outcome pleasing to God
- *After the reading and teaching of the Bible*, to express appropriate responses to what has been heard
- *In a time of intercession*, to pray for a range of people and situations inside and outside the congregation
- *Associated with a baptism or a commissioning for ministry*, to ask for God's care and enabling grace for particular individuals
- *At the conclusion*, to identify important events or activities in the week ahead and to rededicate lives to God's service

---

Summary

Prayer is an aspect of how we, as responsible humans, relate to God as sovereign Lord. In prayer we react to the reality that God has acted of his own will to redeem us and make known his plan and purpose for the whole of creation. In prayer God allows us to be identified with the outworking of his will for his creation. Thus, to the extent that we know him, we 'think his thoughts after him' and our prayer is part of the means by which God achieves his revealed purpose.[11]

The custom of praying 'in Jesus' name' or 'through Jesus Christ our Lord' can be a formality or an empty cliché. But it reflects the important New Testament teaching that we can call God 'Father' only because of the redemptive and intercessory work of the Lord Jesus and the gift of God's Spirit (Rom. 8:14–16; Gal. 4:4–7; Heb. 4:14–16; 7:25). Indeed, Jesus invites us to pray with confidence in his name, when he says, 'I will do whatever you ask in my name, so that the Father may be glorified in the Son' (John 14:13).

Prayer is fundamental to the Christian life and ought therefore to be central to any gathering of Christ's people. It should not be confined to a specified 'prayer time'. Biblically informed prayer, praise and thanksgiving should feature throughout the gathering, linking together the different things we say and do, and enabling the participants to relate every aspect of the service to God.

Biblical prayers and praises should be adapted and used creatively. Spontaneous and informal prayer has a place in our gatherings, but we can also benefit greatly from sharing written prayers together. These may be especially composed for the occasion or come from collections of prayers or liturgies. When his people express themselves in ways that are consistent with biblical revelation, God will be honoured and the church will be edified. Indeed, God's purpose for the world will be advanced when we pray as he has directed.

----

11. These observations are derived from the reflections of
G. Goldsworthy, *Prayer and the Knowledge of God* (Leicester: IVP, 2003), pp. 66–67, 83.

Questions for review and reflection

1. How could the corporate prayer you experience be enriched by your reflecting on the content and pattern of the Lord's Prayer?
2. List some of the ways that prayer could feature more significantly in the pattern of service in your church.
3. What are some of the advantages and disadvantages of using written prayers in our gatherings?
4. What do you find most challenging about the biblical patterns of prayer outlined in this chapter?

7. PRAISING GOD

Praise is an important aspect of human relationships. It is natural to talk about what we admire in others to family and friends, but we also feel the need to express our appreciation to people directly. So, for example, a woman may be praised by those who speak about her qualities to one another, but her husband praises her face to face (Prov. 31:28, 31). Self-praise is inappropriate (Prov. 27:2), and praise of others can be exaggerated, self-serving and even manipulative (Acts 24:2–4).

A genuine relationship with God also involves praise. The psalmists encourage us to praise him directly (8:1–9; 9:1–6; 65:1–13) and to speak about him to others in a way that invites them to acknowledge and glorify him (33:1–11; 47:1–9; 95:1–6). But indirect praise easily leads to direct expressions of appreciation and devotion to God (e.g. 48:1–10; 66:1–15). Christian praise focuses particularly on the Lord Jesus Christ and what he has done for us.

When God's people praise him together, they are stirred to trust and obey him, to hope in him, to love him and to serve him. Our lives should bring praise to God, but the essence of praise in the Bible is speaking or singing about him. As well as being a means of delighting in God and confessing what he is like, praise can function for the edification of the church and as a means for evangelism. So praise can honour God and encourage his people at the same time.

The praises of Israel
Praise words

The Old Testament contains numerous praise terms and many examples of people praising God. The most common Hebrew verb means 'praise, boast, exult' (e.g. Pss 113:1; 117:1–2). It is found in the expression 'hallelujah', meaning 'praise the LORD', which begins and ends numerous psalms (e.g. 135:1, 21; 147:1, 20).[1] The related noun is the Hebrew title for the book we call 'Psalms', indicating that praise is the dominant note in this collection of songs and poems.

Another praise word means 'make music, sing praise' (e.g. Pss 33:2; 98:5; 144:9; 147:7), sometimes with the developed sense of singing to a musical instrument (e.g. 71:22–23).[2] Another term means 'acknowledge, give thanks, praise, confess' (e.g. 118:1, 21; 136:1–3, 26).[3] A sacrifice expressing thanksgiving was sometimes associated with verbal expressions

---

1. The Hebrew verb is *hālal*. Since Jah is an abbreviated form of the special name of God given to Israel (Exod. 3:14; 6:2–3), *hallelujah* is an encouragement to praise the name or character of God.

2. This verb is *zāmar*. A related noun (*mizmôr*) is found in the headings of fifty-seven psalms, indicating that they were to be sung to musical accompaniment. We derive the English term 'psalm' from the Greek *psalmos*, which was used to translate this Hebrew noun.

3. The verb translated 'acknowledge, give thanks, praise, confess' is *yādâ*.

of gratitude by the people of Israel (e.g. 2 Chr. 33:16; Pss 107:22; 116:17; Jon. 2:9).

When God was 'blessed', his people attributed 'blessing' (good qualities and wonderful deeds) to him (e.g. Pss 34:1; 115:18; 117:1; 145:2, 10).[4] When God was 'exalted', his people proclaimed his greatness (e.g. Exod. 15:2; 34:3; Ps. 99:5; Isa. 25:1). When God was 'glorified' or 'honoured' (e.g. Pss 50:15; 86:9, 12; Prov. 3:9; 14:31), his people indicated why glory, honour and praise are due to him (e.g. Pss 96:3; 115:1).[5]

> An individual's song might be a *personal testimony* to God's character and deeds, encouraging others to join in the praise (Pss 145, 146). But some psalms recall the great acts of God experienced by Israel *collectively* and make this the basis for corporate thanksgiving (e.g. 106, 107). Sometimes, when the people of God gathered together, thanks and praise were sung by a choir of Levites (e.g. 1 Chr. 16:4; 2 Chr. 5:13; 31:2; Ezra 3:11; Neh. 12:24). At other times, it would seem that praise was led by individual singers.

Adequate praise

The psalmists sometimes challenge us about how to praise God adequately. There are four significant ways in which they do this. First, a promise such as 'I will praise the LORD all my life; I will sing praise to my God as long as I live' (Ps. 146:2; cf. 111:10; 113:2; 145:2), shows the need for ongoing adoration.

---

4. The verb 'bless' is *bārak*, sometimes translated 'praise', as in Pss 103:1–2, 20–22; 104:1, 35 (NIV).

5. The verb 'exalt' is *rômēm*, and the verb translated 'glorify' or 'honour' is *kābēd*.

Looking for new ways to express familiar truths about God in our songs may help us do this.

Secondly, musical accompaniment is encouraged as a way of reinforcing vocal praise. Trumpets, cymbals, stringed instruments and pipes are mentioned (Pss 92:1–3; 150:3–5). Singing God's praise is associated with rejoicing in the Lord and being glad (32:11; 100:2; 149:1–2). Singing enhances the emotional response of God's people, so that wholehearted praise is offered. The challenge for us is to use instrumental accompaniment creatively to express such praise.

Thirdly, physical expressions of gratitude, joy, enthusiasm, submission and homage are encouraged. Shouting, clapping, lifting the hands, bowing, kneeling and dancing are repeatedly linked to praise (Pss 33:3; 47:1; 95:1–7; 134:2; 149:3). Contemporary churches need to consider how to encourage bodily movement in a way that is culturally relevant and not forced. But rejoicing in God from the heart is clearly meant to be the reality behind such gestures (e.g. 30:11–12; 33:21).

Fourthly, all the nations are summoned to praise God (Pss 66:1, 8; 117:1; 150:6) and the whole created order is summoned to join in (148:1–14).[6] The challenge for Christians is to promote and support the work of the gospel in every land so that the praise of God resounds across the earth.

God-given patterns of praise

Words uttered in praise of God must be truthful, reflecting his self-revelation in word and deed. God's reputation is at stake when his people speak or sing about him to one

---

6. L. C. Allen, 'hll II', in *NIDOTTE*, vol. 1, p. 1036, observes that even inanimate objects can praise God, as they 'fulfil the function assigned to them by the Creator and so witness to his self-revelation through them' (Ps. 19:1–6; Isa. 6:3).

another! Although edification is not mentioned by name, it is implied by the many exhortations in the psalms to praise God together.

David claimed to be inspired by the Spirit of the Lord when he wrote his songs (2 Sam. 23:1–2). His contributions form the basis of the book of Psalms. As we overhear David and the other psalmists speaking to God from their own experiences, we can be confident that these prayers and praises were inspired by God to guide his people in their response to him. We can echo them and also use them as models in our own approach to God, individually and corporately (e.g. Acts 4:25; Rom. 15:9–11).[7]

Singing no doubt took a variety of forms when the Israelites gathered together. Even without musical accompaniment, genuine praise could be spoken by individuals or voiced by a congregation of believers. Some psalms require a response from the congregation (e.g. 136), whereas others may have been sung together (e.g. 147). Some may have been spoken or sung to the congregation to teach and exhort them (e.g. 128).

Some psalms have a complex structure and different 'voices' can be heard as the psalm progresses. So, for example, Psalm 33 begins with an *exhortation* to the righteous to sing joyfully to the Lord and praise him with instrumental accompaniment (vv. 1–3). Then *reasons* for honouring God in this way are given,

7. See B. K. Waltke and J. M. Houston, *The Psalms as Christian Worship: A Historical Commentary* (Grand Rapids: Eerdmans, 2010); J. D. Witvliet, *The Biblical Psalms in Christian Worship: A Brief Introduction and Guide to Resources* (Grand Rapids: Eerdmans, 2007), pp. 16–35.

introduced by the word 'for' (vv. 4–7). An *exhortation* for all the earth to fear the Lord (v. 8) is followed by another set of *reasons*, beginning with 'for' (vv. 9–11). A *blessing* is then pronounced on the nation whose God is the Lord (vv. 12–19). The psalm concludes with a *corporate confession of confidence* in God and a *prayer*, enabling God's people to express their reliance on him (vv. 20–22).

Reasons for praise

Israel's very existence as a nation under God's law was meant to be a testimony to the nations of his character and his will for the world (Deut. 26:18–19; Jer. 13:11). Part of their calling was to proclaim his praise (Ps. 22:23; Isa. 43:21).

According to Psalm 95:1–7, they were to 'sing for joy to the LORD', to 'shout aloud to the Rock of our salvation', to 'come before him with thanksgiving and extol him with music and song'. Two fundamental reasons were given for bowing down in worship and acknowledging him in this way. The first was his identity as 'the great God, the great King above all gods', the only creator and sustainer of everything that exists. The second was his saving activity, which involved choosing and preserving Israel as 'the people of his pasture, the flock under his care' (Ps. 95:7; cf. Exod. 19:5).

Mostly, the Israelites were called to praise God to one another, as a means of encouraging faithfulness and obedience to him. They would honour God in everyday life when their praises were a genuine acknowledgment of what he had revealed about himself (e.g. Pss 34:1–22; 40:1–8). Not just their words, but Israel's character as a holy nation was meant to bring glory to God. So Psalm 95:7–11 challenges those who praise God to keep listening to his voice and not harden their hearts in unbelief or disobedience.

Psalm 95 has been very influential in Christian circles. The warning to hear God's voice with belief and obedience is picked up in Hebrews 3:7 – 4:13. The invitation to come before God with thanksgiving and extol him with music and song has been echoed in numerous versions of the psalm written for Christians to sing together. The psalm as a whole features as a regular 'call to worship' in a number Christian liturgies. It suggests a natural bridge from praise to the hearing of God's word.

Sometimes Old Testament believers had opportunities to praise God in the company of unbelievers (e.g. Dan. 2:27–45; 3:16–18; Jon. 1:7–9; 3:1–6). Their testimony was a form of praise because it proclaimed the truth about God and called upon foreigners to recognize and honour him. In Christian terms, sharing the gospel with people and testifying to his work in your life is a means of praising God (Heb. 13:15).

In Psalm 96 the challenge for Israel was to 'declare his glory among the nations, his marvellous deeds among all peoples' (v. 3). This was in the context of the psalmist's invitation to 'sing to the LORD, all the earth' (v. 1). God desires that the nations should acknowledge his greatness, 'come into his courts' and 'worship the LORD in the splendour of his holiness' (vv. 8–9). God's people were to testify that 'The LORD reigns' and that 'he comes to judge the earth' (vv. 10–13).

The New Testament points to the fulfilment of this hope in the preaching of the gospel to the nations, which gathers believers from everywhere to worship with believing Israelites at God's heavenly throne (e.g. Rom. 15:7–12; Heb. 12:22–24; Rev. 7:9–17; 14:6–7).

Christian praise
Acknowledging the fulfilment of God's saving plan

New expressions of praise pour from the lips of those who witness the births of John the Baptist and Jesus in Luke 1 – 2. Language familiar to us from the Old Testament is used in their songs, as God is glorified for bringing the promised messianic salvation to Israel. These prophetic outbursts anticipate the praise of the Spirit-filled community of believers in Jerusalem after Jesus' ascension (Acts 2:46–47; 4:24–28), and the praise of people from many nations who then respond to their proclamation about the exalted Lord (10:44–46; 13:48). The songs in Luke 1 – 2 have found their way into Christian liturgies, to be recited together, and have also been adapted for singing in various forms.

New Testament letters sometimes reveal patterns of praise embedded in the writer's argument.[8] For example, Paul pauses to glorify God at Romans 1:25 ('the Creator – who is for ever praised'), 9:5 ('the Messiah, who is God over all, for ever praised') and 16:27 ('to the only wise God be glory for ever through Jesus Christ!'). More extensively, Paul concludes Romans 9 – 11 with a blessing, as he reflects on God's sovereign grace in choosing, calling and saving the people of the New Covenant from Israel and the nations:

> Oh, the depth of the riches of the wisdom and knowledge of God!
> How unsearchable his judgments,

---

8. Scholars debate whether there are fragments of early Christian hymns incorporated in passages such as Phil. 2:6–11; Col. 1:15–20; 1 Tim. 3:16. See R. P. Martin, 'Hymns, Hymn Fragments, Songs, Spiritual Songs', in G. F. Hawthorne, R. P. Martin and D. G. Reid (eds.), *Dictionary of Paul and His Letters* (Downers Grove: InterVarsity Press; Leicester: Inter-Varsity Press, 1993), pp. 419–423.

and his paths beyond tracing out!
'Who has known the mind of the Lord?
    Or who has been his counsellor'?
'Who has ever given to God,
    that God should repay them?'
For from him and through him and for him are all things.
To him be the glory for ever! Amen.
(11:33–36)

> Paul marvels at the wisdom and knowledge of God in bringing
> his great plan of salvation to fulfilment. But he admits that we
> are limited in our understanding of God's ways to what he
> reveals about himself. With an allusion to Isaiah 40:13 and Job
> 41:11 he acknowledges that human beings cannot know the mind
> of the Lord, give him advice or oblige him to repay them in any
> way. These admissions lead to a doxology or expression of the
> praise due to God (Rom. 11:36). Paul's example here encourages
> us to incorporate biblical phrases and allusions in our praise and
> to be enthusiastic in proclaiming his glory to one another.

Such praise follows the Old Testament pattern of blessing
God for his character and actions (e.g. Gen. 14:20; 1 Sam.
25:32; 2 Sam. 18:28). We find other forms of Christian blessing
in 2 Corinthians 1:3–4, Ephesians 1:3–14 and 1 Peter 1:3–9,
where God is praised in exalted language for his saving activity.
In these passages the authors include themselves with the
readers as recipients of the blessings outlined.[9]

---

9. All forms of declarative praise are called *běrākâ* (the Hebrew for
   'blessing'). See n. 4 above on blessing God and P. T. O'Brien, *The
   Letter to the Ephesians*, PNTC (Grand Rapids: Eerdmans; Leicester:
   Apollos, 1999), pp. 89–90.

Three times in Ephesian 1:3–14 it is indicated that God has acted to bring about the praise of his glory (1:6, 12, 14). Father, Son and Holy Spirit have contributed to the accomplishment of our salvation and should be praised by our response in word and deed. 1 Peter 1:3–9 is comprehensive in a different way. Its focus is on the resurrection of Jesus and its implications for Christians now and in the life to come. These passages can be adapted for use in praising God together.

Praise and godly living

Praise is meant to be an identifying mark of the new people of God. Christians are to 'declare the praises of him who called you out of darkness into his marvellous light' (1 Pet. 2:9). As in the Old Testament, singing about God to one another is an important way of doing this, though the inspiration now is specifically 'the message of Christ' (Col. 3:16–17) and the Spirit's role in this ministry is highlighted (Eph. 5:18–20). The need for a lifestyle that brings honour and praise to God is stressed in many passages (e.g. Rom. 15:7; 1 Cor. 6:20; 2 Cor. 9:11–13; Phil. 1:11; 1 Pet. 1:7; 3:15). Corporate praise should encourage praise in everyday-life situations.

As previously noted, the 'sacrifice of praise' that Christians can offer to God through Jesus is 'the fruit of lips that openly profess his name' (Heb. 13:15). This confessing of the 'name' or character of God can take place in the fellowship of believers and in the world. Verbal praise can take the form of testimony, proclamation or song. The praise passages we have noted suggest the need for profound and extensive declarations of God's glory, showing how he has 'blessed us in the heavenly realms with every spiritual blessing in Christ' (Eph. 1:3).

Miroslav Volf observes:

> In thanking, blessing or praising God, a person expresses his or
> her own relation to the God he or she is adoring: joyous *gratitude*
> for what God has done and reverent *alignment* with God's
> character from which God's actions spring forth.[10]

Praise strengthens us in our relationship with God. Volf
also argues that adoration is the 'well-spring of action',
because it is a way of aligning ourselves with God's character
and purposes and expressing a desire to be 'a co-operator
with God in the world'. Adoration is the context that gives
meaning to our actions, because 'adoration identifies the God
in whose name one engages in action'.[11] Actions done in the
name of God then lead others to praise him (Matt. 5:16;
2 Cor. 4:15; 9:11; 1 Pet. 2:11). So a circle of adoration and
action is generated:

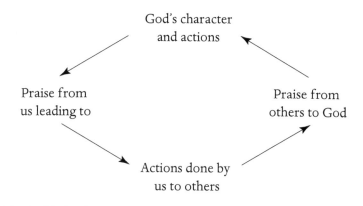

---

10. M. Volf, 'Worship as Adoration and Action: Reflections on a Christian
    Way of Being-in-the-World', in D. A. Carson (ed.), *Worship: Adoration
    and Action*, World Evangelical Fellowship (Grand Rapids: Baker;
    Exeter: Paternoster, 1993), p. 210 (original emphasis).
11. Ibid.

Anticipating the end

The Revelation to John portrays the unceasing worship of those gathered around the throne of God in heaven. Homage is offered to God and to the Lamb by heavenly beings and by redeemed men and women, with words of acclamation and praise (Rev. 4:10; 5:14; 7:11; 11:16; 15:4; 19:4). However, despite this interest in heavenly worship, John also concentrates on the earthly scene. Various forms of idolatry are portrayed (9:20; 13:4, 8, 12), together with prophecies of the awful judgment coming upon those who bow to false gods and refuse to acknowledge the living and true God.[12]

Glimpses of the final destination of God's people are interspersed in this book with visions of judgment to encourage the readers to endure patiently and be faithful in the present. Those who are redeemed from the earth sing various songs before the throne of God and serve him day and night (7:9–17). The implication is that only those who abstain from false worship on earth will share, by God's grace, in the worship of heaven.

- As in the Old Testament, this heavenly praise generally involves a *description* of what God has done, as well as an *expression* of thanksgiving or glory.
- Descriptions are normally introduced by the words 'for' or 'because' (4:11; 5:9–10; 11:17–18; 15:4; 19:2).
- Adoration is expressed in words such as 'You are worthy, our Lord and God, to receive glory and honour and

---

12. I have discussed this more fully in *Engaging with God: A Biblical Theology of Worship* (Leicester: Apollos; Downers Grove: InterVarsity Press, 1992), pp. 261–270.

power' (4:11), or 'We give thanks to you, Lord God
Almighty, the One who is and who was' (11:17),
or 'Great and marvellous are your deeds, Lord God
Almighty. Just and true are your ways, King of the
nations. Who will not fear you, Lord, and bring
glory to your name?' (15:3–4), or 'Hallelujah!
Salvation and glory and power belong to our God'
(19:1).

- But profound reasons are given for speaking to God
in this way.

In Revelation 4:8–11 God is praised as the utterly holy and
eternal creator and preserver of everything that exists. Then
the one who sits at God's right hand is identified as 'the Lion
of the tribe of Judah, the Root of David', who has triumphed
(5:1–5). Such biblical language clearly points to Jesus as the
promised messianic king. He is also identified as 'a Lamb,
looking as if it had been slain', and praise is offered to him for
bringing into existence the new people of God by means of
his sacrificial death (5:6–10). In 5:11–14 he is worshipped and
praised in a way that parallels the homage paid to God in
Revelation 4.

Praise and glory offered to God and the Lamb in Revelation
7:10–16 focus on the way believers have been brought through
'the great tribulation' to enjoy the blessings of God's eternal
kingdom. With the sounding of the last trumpet, loud voices
in heaven proclaim that

The kingdom of the world has become
    the kingdom of our Lord and of his Messiah,
and he will reign for ever and ever.
(11:15)

This provokes the twenty-four elders, seated on their thrones before God, to fall on their faces and pay homage to God with an outburst of thanksgiving (11:17–18).

> The heavenly court is grateful because God has exercised his powerful rule over rebellious men and women by inaugurating the final judgment (see 16:5–7; 19:1–5). But they also rejoice that God will bring people from every nation to worship at his throne in heaven (15:3–4) and to share in 'the wedding of the Lamb' (19:6–9).

Rejoicing in God and his victory, giving him the glory and praising him are all different aspects of the homage or worship that is due to him. Adoration and praise occur in the Revelation to John as the events of the end time are unfolded or as they are anticipated. Adoration and praise also look back to the saving work of God in Christ and spell out all its benefits.

Reflecting on the songs we sing

The doxologies, acclamations and hymns of praise in the Revelation to John have found their way into many Christian songs and liturgies throughout the centuries. This has happened because of the form as well as the content of these segments. With the greatest of ease they can be adapted for congregational use. But it would be simplistic to say that Revelation was written to encourage churches on earth to imitate the actions of the heavenly assembly or to sing the same songs.

What is needed above all is to reflect the same confidence in God and the outworking of his plan for his people. Christ on the throne of heaven reminds the church today that our gospel message about his death, resurrection and ascension should be the focus of our life now and for ever.

Revelation certainly suggests that praising God together is an important Christian activity. It is a powerful way of affirming fundamental gospel truths and of acknowledging God's gracious rule over creation and history. Together with teaching and various forms of exhortation, appropriate praise can strengthen Christians to maintain their confidence in God and in the outworking of his purposes in a world devoted to idolatry and every kind of God-rejecting activity. Testifying to the goodness and power of God in the congregation of his people can be a means of encouraging such testimony before unbelievers in everyday life.

A careful study of the pattern of praise in the New Testament should cause us to reflect on the content and style of the praise we use in our gatherings. Contemporary songwriters and those who choose our songs should help us grasp the breadth and depth of what is revealed there. What is missing from the hymns and songs sung in the church to which you belong?

- Do they major on praising God for his character and his mighty acts in history on our behalf?
- Do they draw us to the great truths of the gospel?
- Is the choice of songs too narrowly focused on only one aspect of the gospel?
- Does the language we use appropriately reflect the power and meaning of the language used in biblical forms of praise?
- Do our hymns and songs help us to rejoice in God's gracious and powerful rule, acknowledge its blessings and look forward to its consummation in the new creation?

- Do they challenge us to take a firm stand against every manifestation of evil and to bear faithful witness to the truth of the gospel in our society?

Summary

From Genesis to Revelation praise is offered to God individually and corporately. It is said or sung to God directly or expressed indirectly, even as his people challenge one another to extol his virtues. There are many praise words in the Bible and most of them indicate the need to confess, to acknowledge, to extol or to give thanks for who God is, as revealed in his words and actions.

Praise is more than saying 'Hallelujah' or repeating praise mantras. It involves articulating what makes God praiseworthy. This is sometimes described as exalting God or magnifying him. Both of these terms imply some way of proclaiming his virtues for others to appreciate. Commending God to one another promotes faith, hope and love. But praise should also be addressed to God personally.

Praise is meant to be vigorous and heart-felt because the gospel is such great news. Consequently, the value of musical accompaniment is stressed and bodily movement in association with praise is encouraged. The call for the nations to praise God picks up God's concern to bless the nations (Gen. 12:3) and is a challenge for his people to speak and act in ways that display his character and will to unbelievers.

Personal testimony or public preaching about God should express praise, inviting others to praise him as well. Although some biblical praise was sung by believers together, individual singers and choirs seem to have had a significant role in Old Testament gatherings for worship. This pattern suggests that there is a place in our gatherings also for corporate singing, for individuals ministering in song and for choirs.

Christian praise highlights the faithfulness of God in fulfilling his promises and sending his Son to be the promised
messianic saviour and ruler of the nations. It focuses on the
implications of Jesus' death, resurrection and ascension for
believers. It proclaims in advance the coming judgment of
God and the return of Christ to consummate God's plans for
his people.

Praise provides Christians with the opportunity to confess
together what they believe about God. So it becomes a way
of realigning ourselves with his character and will. Praise
edifies the church and encourages faithfulness to God in
everyday living. But it also challenges unbelievers about the
need to glorify God and give thanks to him.

Questions for review and reflection

1. Why is it important to take note of the 'for' and
   'because' statements associated with biblical forms of
   praise?
2. How can we encourage more sincere and meaningful
   praise in our churches?
3. What might be the advantages of speaking, rather than
   singing, praise to God?
4. How might some of the biblical songs of praise be
   adapted or used to edify our churches?

8. SINGING TOGETHER

As noted in the last chapter, singing is a significant way of expressing heartfelt adoration and thanksgiving to God, individually and corporately. But songs can also be vehicles for prayer or be used to instruct and exhort one another (Col. 3:16). Singing has great potential for uniting and edifying the church (1 Cor. 14:15–17), though sadly it is sometimes a cause of division and alienation. In many congregations there is continuing debate about 'what music will be sung, what style it will be, who will lead it, what instruments will be used, and how loud it will be'.[1]

It is easy to think about music in quite selfish terms: 'This is what I like and every other kind of music is unsatisfying and

---

1. J. D. Witvliet, 'Beyond Style: Rethinking the Role of Music in Worship', in T. E. Johnson (ed.), *The Conviction of Things Not Seen: Worship and Ministry in the 21st Century* (Grand Rapids: Brazo, 2002), p. 68. Witvliet goes on to discuss six questions that congregations should address when seeking to answer these questions.

unattractive for me.' We all have musical tastes and some of us are quite strong in articulating them! Preferences for traditional hymns, modern hymns, or songs that adapt contemporary styles such as rock, pop, folk or country are often linked to fond recollections of meaningful spiritual experiences. Getting people to try something new can be like asking them to forget their favourite memories.

Since music is sometimes in the 'too hard basket', churches develop different gatherings, with distinct music styles, to keep as many people as possible happy. There may be other reasons for having separate gatherings, but when these are identified by musical taste, we encourage congregations to define themselves by personal preference, rather than in biblical terms. How can we express our unity in Christ at the level of musical expression?

If singing is to be a unifying and encouraging part of our church life, we need to apply the Scriptures to this ministry in a rigorous fashion for the benefit of musicians, song leaders and congregations. Issues of content, style, presentation, balance and the placement of songs within a service are critical. Leadership in this ministry, as in other areas of church life, demands appropriate training and support for those involved.

Honouring God
False trails

Although it is sometimes suggested that only certain types of music can honour God, the Bible gives us no guidance about this. False or meaningless words dishonour God, but Scripture does not reveal the kind of music God prefers! Value judgments about the style of music we choose can-not be the deciding factor. The principle of 'the best to honour God' can be applied to all sorts of music. So we should do whatever we do well and not confuse quality with style.[2]

Another line of argument suggests we need music that will lift us up to God and help us to worship him appropriately. Only certain types of music are said to be 'elevating' and able to take us outside ourselves to God. Put another way, some would argue that music should help us experience more of God and get closer to him. But such an approach implies that we need to do something to open the channel of communication with God. Even vigorous praise cannot do this.[3]

In biblical teaching the initiative lies with God, not with us. We can certainly pray that he would move us to honour him and encourage one another in our singing. But God's ability to minister to us in a gathering of his people does not depend on the intensity of our singing, the degree of our enthusiasm or the style of our music.

Listening and responding to God

The New Testament teaches that there was a three-way movement in the early church's meetings: from God to his people, from the people to God and from the members of the congregation to one another. Howard Marshall says:

---

2. B. Kauflin, *Worship Matters: Leading Others to Encounter the Greatness of God* (Wheaton: Crossway, 2008), pp. 33–41, offers helpful comments on the development of musical skills and considers why this is important for church musicians.

3. Witvliet, 'Beyond Style', pp. 71–73, observes that 'music has great significance in the divine–human encounter of worship', but rightly argues against the view that music or singing can generate an experience of God.

The primary element is the God–man movement, downward rather than upward, in which God comes to his people and uses his human servants to convey his salvation to them, to strengthen and upbuild them. He bestows his charismata in order to equip the members of the church to serve one another. Of course, the effect of such service by God to his people will be to move them to praise, thanksgiving and prayer, but the point is that this is *response* and is secondary to what is primary, namely the flow of divine grace.[4]

I see it like this:

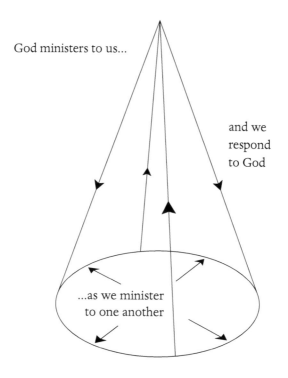

God ministers to us...

and we respond to God

...as we minister to one another

---

4. I. H. Marshall, 'How Far Did the Early Christians *Worship* God?', *Chm* 99 (1985), p. 227 (my emphasis).

Music can be a significant contributor to each aspect of a gathering. As we address one another in songs about biblical truths, God's Spirit may give us fresh insights and a renewed desire to serve him. Songs can also be used to express repentance, faith or praise to God. Some songs are more obviously directed to God, and others to one another, but both types can function to remind us of what he has revealed to us, while enabling us to respond to him.

The three 'movements' can take place during the singing of the same song. Take the first verse of Charles Wesley's famous hymn as an example:

And can it be that I should gain
*   an interest in the Saviour's blood?*
Died he for me, who caused his pain –
*   for me, who him to death pursued?*
Amazing love! how can it be
*   that thou my God shoulds't die for me!*

The corporate movement takes place as we remind each other to consider the grace of God in the death of Christ and its significance for us personally (see Ps. 103). God's Spirit may apply the message to many hearts as we minister to one another in this way. Self-reflection leads us to praise God directly for his amazing love ('how can it be that thou my God shoulds't die for me!').

Colossians 3:16 brings the three-way movement to clear expression: 'Let the message of Christ dwell among you richly as you teach and admonish one another with all wisdom through psalms, hymns and songs from the Spirit, singing to God with gratitude in your hearts.'

God ministers to us as 'the message of Christ' begins to inhabit and control every aspect of our lives together.[5] This happens as the gospel is taught and applied in different ways, even through singing. Paul links the horizontal dimension of singing ('teach and admonish one another with all wisdom through psalms, hymns and songs from the Spirit') with the vertical response ('singing to God with gratitude in your hearts'). Paul also indicates that this ministry should be conducted 'with all wisdom'.

Ministry with wisdom

In contrast with the wisdom claimed by certain first-century false teachers (Col. 2:23), Paul insisted that 'all the treasures of wisdom and knowledge' are found in Christ (2:3). The apostle taught 'with all wisdom', so as to 'present everyone fully mature in Christ' (1:28). He also prayed that his converts would be filled with the knowledge of God's will 'through all the wisdom and understanding that the Spirit gives', so that they might 'live a life worthy of the Lord and please him in every way' (1:9–10).

The teaching and admonition that Christians give to one another is meant to follow Paul's example and express Christ-centred, Spirit-directed, life-changing wisdom (3:16). Consider what this means for the content of our songs. Consider also what it means for the way we minister to one another in song and the outcome we seek from singing together. The phrase 'with all wisdom' can apply to each of these concerns.

Rather than focusing on subjective experiences of God or personal needs, Christian songs should express the wisdom

---

5. 'The message of Christ' is literally 'the word about Christ' (*ho logos tou Christou*), 'the true message of the gospel' that has come to the Colossians and is bearing fruit among them (1:5–6). See P. T. O'Brien, *Colossians, Philemon*, WBC 44 (Waco: Word, 1982), pp. 206–207.

that God has revealed to us in Christ for our salvation, maturation and fruitfulness in his service (see 1 Cor. 1:18–31; 2:6–16;
Eph. 1:17). The phrase 'with all wisdom' in Colossians 3:16
may also suggest that 'the teaching and admonition are given
in a thoughtful and tactful manner'.[6] Furthermore, if our
songs truly reflect the 'understanding that the Spirit gives'
(1:9), they will convey wisdom for godly living. Christian song-
writers should pray for such wisdom as they compose. Those
who select songs for congregational ministry and those who
plan and lead church services should also seek the Spirit's
wisdom for their task.

Paul's challenge in a parallel passage is to 'be filled with the
Spirit, speaking to one another with psalms, hymns and songs
from the Spirit' (Eph. 5:18–19). This address to the whole
congregation comes in the context of a warning to be wise
about how to live and to 'understand what the Lord's will is'
(5:15–17). Wisdom and the Spirit are closely linked once more.

> The sequence of clauses in Ephesians 5:18–21 suggests that
> 'Spirit-filled Christians are people whose lives are characterized
> by singing, thanksgiving, and mutual submission.'[7] God is
> bringing his people to fullness of life in Christ or maturity as
> they participate in the edification of his church (4:11–16). The
> Spirit enables them to play their part in this process, even as

---

6. Ibid., p. 208. See Col. 4:5.

7. P. T. O'Brien, *The Letter to the Ephesians*, PNTC (Grand Rapids:
   Eerdmans; Leicester: Apollos, 1999), p. 388. He notes that the
   present imperative in the Greek text (*plērousthe*, 'be filled') suggests
   that the Spirit's infilling of Christians is to be continual. In view of
   Eph. 1:23, 3:19, 4:10–13, the Spirit mediates to believers 'the fullness
   of God and Christ'.

they sing together, give thanks to God and submit to one
another. Put another way, 'we are to be subject to the Spirit's
control (see 1:17; 3:16), which is tantamount to letting Christ's
word rule in our lives'.[8]

Psalms, hymns and songs from the Spirit

Paul refers to 'psalms, hymns and songs from the Spirit' in
Ephesians 5:19 and Colossians 3:16.[9] Both verses highlight the
way singing can be a form of ministry to one another. The
vertical dimension is expressed in Ephesians 5:19 when he says
(literally), 'singing and making music with your heart to the
Lord' (cf. Ps. 111:1).

The 'heart' signifies the whole person in biblical psychology
(see Deut. 6:5; Rom. 5:5; 6:17). Paul does not simply refer to an
inward disposition when he talks about singing and making
music 'with your heart': 'the entire person should be filled
with songs of praise, thereby expressing the reality of life in
the Spirit'.[10] Music and singing have the potential to involve the
whole person in prayer and praise.

Singing 'with my spirit' and 'with my understanding'
(1 Cor. 14:15–17) may similarly be a way of describing the
participation of the whole person in the act of singing. Paul
wants the Corinthians to pray and sing with mind and spirit

---

8. Ibid., p. 393. Singing together is a way of edifying the church,
making melody to the Lord and of being filled with the Spirit.

9. Most English versions translate the expression *ōdais pneumatikais*
literally as 'spiritual songs', but the NIV (2011) has 'songs from the
Spirit'. This is justifiable in view of Paul's focus on the Spirit's role in
this ministry (Eph. 5:19) and the parallel focus on the word's ruling
through Spirit-directed wisdom (Col. 1:9–12; 3:16).

10. O' Brien, *Ephesians*, p. 396.

together for the edification of the church. But some would describe 'singing with my spirit' as a novel and distinct form of Christian music – a way of 'singing in tongues'. If this is correct, the contrast between praying and singing 'with my spirit' and 'with my understanding' aims at 'relegating the former to the setting of private praying, while only the latter is to be exercised in the assembly'.[11] Paul insists that what is sung in church should be immediately intelligible to all who are present and therefore edifying.

The three terms 'psalms', 'hymns' and 'songs' occur interchangeably in the titles of psalms in the Old Testament. So firm distinctions cannot be drawn between them and no exact classification of New Testament song material can be made on this basis. Taken together, however, these terms describe 'the full range of singing which the Spirit prompts'.[12] Consistent with the Spirit's role in testifying about the Son and glorifying him (John 15:26; 16:14), songs that can be gleaned from the New Testament focus on Christ and the fulfilment of God's purpose for Israel and the nations in him.[13]

---

11. G. D. Fee, *The First Epistle to the Corinthians*, NICNT (Grand Rapids: Eerdmans, 1987), p. 671. Fee envisages the possibility that 'spontaneous hymns of praise were offered to God in the congregation, although some may have been known beforehand'. However, he rightly insists that Paul opposes unintelligible singing and praying in the setting of corporate worship.

12. E. Lohse, *Colossians and Philemon* (Philadelphia: Fortress, 1971), p. 151. See O'Brien, *Ephesians*, pp. 395–396; K. H. Bartels, 'Song, Hymn, Psalm', *NIDNTT*, vol. 3, pp. 668–676.

13. See chapter 7, n. 8, regarding possible fragments of early Christian hymns in various New Testament passages. Most obviously, the songs in Luke 1 – 2 and the Revelation to John focus on Christ and the fulfilment of God's purpose through him.

Old Testament songs were no doubt used as models by the earliest Christians to suit various needs and situations (see Acts 4:24–30; Heb. 3:7–15; Rev. 15:3–4). But new compositions soon emerged in different contexts. There is remarkable evidence from a letter written in about AD 112 that Christians in Asia Minor met 'on a fixed day to assemble before daylight and recite by turns a form of words to Christ as a god'.[14] This probably refers to their singing together to honour their Lord.

Music, singing and edification

Edification is the missing factor in much of our thinking about music and singing. The biblical theology of edification examined in chapter 3 is our best guide in evaluating and developing a ministry of 'psalms, hymns and songs from the Spirit'.

Possibilities and problems

Music makes it possible for a number of people to exercise their gifts for the edification of the church. As instrumentalists join together to accompany the singing, as individuals or groups sing to encourage the congregation, and as the people of God sing together about what they believe, there can be a powerful expression of the unity we have in Christ. 'The message of Christ' is brought to bear on our lives in a significant way (Col. 3:16), we are moved towards maturity in Christ (Eph. 4:13), we have the opportunity to praise God together (Rom. 15:8–11) and we are challenged to serve

---

14. Pliny, who was the Roman governor of Bythynia, wrote this to the emperor Trajan in Rome. See J. Stevensen (ed.), *A New Eusebius: Documents Illustrative of the History of the Church to AD 337* (London: SPCK. 1963), p. 14.

him with gratitude in every sphere of life (Eph. 5:20; Col. 3:17).

Participation in the prayers and praises of the church is an expression of our common participation in Christ and the benefits of his saving work. But a musical style may be unfamiliar or difficult for some people to appreciate. If tunes are not well chosen or if some find the musical accompaniment inappropriate or distracting, the process of edification may be hindered. Additionally, if songs are played badly, the congregation will probably not be edified. Some may be confused or annoyed by the music so that they cannot participate wholeheartedly in the singing. In effect, they cannot say 'Amen' and so feel alienated (see 1 Cor. 14:15–17).

> All church music should have the ability to speak to the entire congregation. If the music is divisive, if most of the people do not understand what is happening, if it does not have meaning to most, then it is probably improper and wrong.[15]

As already noted, Christians can be very subjective and strongly opinionated about what constitutes 'good music'. Pastors and song leaders need to be sensitive to the cultural context, aesthetic taste, musical expectations and spiritual maturity of each congregation in their care.

Those responsible for choosing songs should have a special concern for the sense and intention of the words. Are they archaic or too theologically complex? Are they simplistic and lacking in sufficient biblical content? Song leaders should also take account of the musical experience and skill of the congregation when introducing new songs. Is the tune difficult

---

15. A. C. Lovelace and W. C. Rice, *Music and Worship in the Church*, rev. ed. (Nashville: Abingdon, 1976), p. 203.

to sing or is this group of people unfamiliar with the style of music and how it should be sung?[16]

Some may resist change because they lack confidence musically or because no one has helped them appreciate the value of learning new songs for their own growth or for the benefit of the congregation. Variety should be encouraged, not simply for its own sake but to encourage spiritual vitality and the maturation of the church.

Those who plan church services should consider carefully the function of songs at particular stages in the meeting. Here are some possibilities to consider:

- Do the opening songs help us focus on the character of God and why we should praise him together?
- Is there a song that articulates our confidence before God through the gospel?
- Do any of the songs enable us to express repentance?
- Is there a song that challenges us to listen carefully to the Bible readings and sermon?
- Does the song after the ministry of the word help the people to respond to what they have heard then and there?
- Are there ever songs through which we pray for others?
- Is there a song of dedication and commitment to serve God in the week that lies ahead?

With sufficient preparation and help older Christians can learn to appreciate contemporary music. Younger Christians

---

16. M. Evans, *Open up the Doors: Music in the Modern Church* (London: Equinox, 2006), provides help in evaluating contemporary Christian music forms.

can also be put in touch with the contributions and insights of former generations. If introduced appropriately, there is a rich treasury of hymns from across the centuries that can serve our needs today and provide what is lacking in modern songs. Of course, the reverse is also true: some modern music expresses biblical truth that is hardly emphasized in older material.[17]

On a wider scale, we need to discover how Christians from different races and cultures have expressed themselves in song to God. Song structures, musical style and instrumentation will vary. Learning to enjoy such variety is a way of experiencing the breadth of Christian experience beyond the limitations of our own context.

Working together

As with other ministries in the church, music directors and song leaders should be chosen and appointed carefully. As well as having musical gifts they should be mature Christians and be able to give spiritual leadership to those in their care. The whole church should be taught how to share insights and preferences about musical contributions for the benefit of the body, not just as a means of self-expression. Here, as in other areas of ministry, we need to be 'speaking the truth in love', which is essential to the process of edification (see Eph. 4:15–16).

Music leaders should encourage singers and musicians to study the Bible and pray together, to develop mature relationships and godly goals for ministry. They should also expose

17. A history of Christian music can be found in A. Wilson-Dickson, *The Story of Christian Music: From Gregorian Chant to Black Gospel, an Authoritative Illustrated Guide to All the Major Traditions of Music for Worship* (Oxford: Lion, 1992).

themselves to peer group review and feedback from the congregation from time to time, to discover how their ministry is impacting the lives of others.[18]

Pastors need to consider how best to work with musicians in the development of the ministry and in the process of choosing music and teaching new songs.[19] Much will depend on the musical competency of the pastor. Those with little experience need to take advice in a humble way, while still exercising oversight of congregational meetings and their content. Pastors who are musically competent must be careful not to take over the leadership of the music and undermine the authority of those appointed to this role.

Music and the emotions

Music can touch our emotions and speak to the deep recesses of our personalities. At concerts, films, sporting events and political gatherings music can move us to tears, make us smile or inspire loyalty to some cause or personality.[20] Especially when associated with words that have social or historical significance, music can bind people together and give them a 'spiritual' experience. But Christians need to be careful about identifying comparable events in a Christian context with the presence of God and the work of his Spirit.

Being moved emotionally is not identical with being moved by the Spirit of God. 'Music affects and helps us in many ways,

---

18. Kauflin, *Worship Matters*, pp. 213–248, addresses many aspects of musical leadership in churches.

19. Kauflin, ibid., pp. 249–259, offers some helpful thoughts for pastors with regard to the music ministry in their churches.

20. See R. Smith, 'Music, Singing and the Emotions: Exploring the Connections', in M. P. Jensen (ed.), *True Feelings: Perspectives on Emotions in Christian Life and Ministry* (Nottingham: IVP, 2012), pp. 254–277.

but it doesn't replace truth about God . . . Good theology helps us keep music in its proper place.'[21] If music is simply used to create a mood or to entertain, it can be manipulative (e.g. the excessive repetition of songs to intensify the emotions of those present). But when it is employed to highlight the meaning of words, music can plant biblical truth memorably and powerfully in our hearts. Music can help us to be involved in prayer and praise emotionally as well as intellectually. It can be a vehicle for expressing deep reflections and feelings.

> Music is a language in its own right, and, as an art, a means of communication. Using pitches, rhythms, harmonies, timbres, and form it is as capable today of running the gamut of emotions from exaltation through gaiety, joy, excitement, solemnity, and fear to extreme dejection and sorrow as it was in the days of the biblical singers – Miriam, David and Zechariah.[22]

The best congregational songs are those where biblical truth is beautifully expressed and enhanced by appropriate music, where tunes are not awkward to sing, so that they distract from the words, and the structure is balanced and easy to follow. Instrumentation and arrangement can also have a big impact on the way a congregation engages with a song. Some songs can have a different emphasis with a different tune.

It is important as well to distinguish between emotions and emotionalism in singing together.

> Some Christians repress their emotions as they sing. They fear feeling everything too strongly and think maturity means holding back. But the problem is *emotionalism*, not *emotions*. Emotionalism

---

21. Kauflin, *Worship Matters*, p. 30.
22. Lovelace and Rice, *Music and Worship*, p. 16.

pursues feelings as an end in themselves. It's wanting to feel something with no regard for how that feeling is produced or its ultimate purpose. Emotionalism can also view heightened emotions as the infallible sign that God is present. In contrast, the emotions that singing is meant to invoke are a response to who God is and what he's done. Vibrant singing enables us to combine truth *about* God seamlessly with passion *for* God.[23]

Emotions give no clear indication of the genuineness of the heart's commitment or of the Holy Spirit's power and presence. But biblical teaching suggests that emotion is an important aspect of our personalities and therefore part of our response to God. Our physiological and psychological individuality will mean that emotions are excited and expressed differently, even when confronted by the same stimuli in a given context. Emotionalism clearly goes beyond biblical teaching by making the pursuit of feelings an end in itself and by identifying heightened emotions with the presence of God.

Summary

Singing together can help us remember and respond to biblical teaching about God and his will for our lives. God's Spirit may move songwriters to express biblical truth in new and challenging ways, so God can minister to us as we sing to one another about what he has revealed to us. Singing together can also be a way of responding to God with repentance, faith and praise. Music helps us to express God-glorifying emotion, when it accompanies and highlights the meaning of appropriate words. Singing together and playing music for the glory

---

23. Kauflin, *Worship Matters*, p. 99 (original emphasis). See D. G. Peterson, 'Together, with Feeling: Corporate Worship and the Emotions', in Jensen, *True Feelings*, pp. 235–253.

of God and the edification of the church can help us mature in Christ.

The glory of the gospel is to unite peoples of every language and culture under the lordship of Christ (Eph. 2:11–22; 4:3–6, 13; Rev. 7:9–17). So we should not be content with divisions created by different musical tastes and traditions. As we grow to maturity in Christ we should be looking for ways to express the unity that is God's goal for us: in gospel action, in the exchange of ministries and gifts, in combined services and in the sharing of musical resources and experiences.

A vital music ministry will be possible only when pastors, music directors and their teams are working together in harmony, modelling biblical teaching about edification. Music directors or song leaders need to have a pastoral approach to the whole church, exhibiting warmth and humility and being able to inspire confidence about singing together, learning new songs and enjoying the contributions of musicians and singers.

Questions for review and reflection

1. How could you tell if a music ministry was being conducted 'with all wisdom' (Col. 3:16)?
2. What does it mean in practical terms to be 'filled with the Spirit' as we speak to one another 'with psalms, hymns and songs from the Spirit' (Eph. 5:18–19)?
3. How might singing hinder or help the edification of the church?
4. Why might it be helpful to have a variety of musical styles and song traditions in a gathering?

9. BAPTISM

Baptism in the New Testament is part of the process of bringing people to Christ and making them his disciples (Matt. 28:19–20). In obedience to the command of Jesus, the salvation promised in the gospel was proclaimed by the apostles and received by many through baptism with repentance and faith (Acts 2:38–39). Those who were drawn to the Lord in this way were added to his church (Acts 2:41–47). Although some baptisms in the New Testament took place in isolation (Acts 8:36–38; 9:17–18), others were more public (Acts 10:44–48; 16:14–15, 32–34).

Different theologies of baptism emerged across the centuries, dividing Christians over a practice that is supposed to unite them.[1] As we consider biblical teaching and touch on various baptismal traditions, the aim will be to reflect on what may unite believers and edify the church. According to

---

1. See J. H. Armstrong and P. E. Engle (eds.), *Understanding Four Views on Baptism* (Grand Rapids: Zondervan, 2009).

Ephesians 4:1–6, we are to express and maintain that unity of the Spirit implied by the confession of 'one Lord, one faith, one baptism; one God and Father of all, who is over all and through all and in all'.

The baptism of John
In the New Testament John the Baptist appears as the promised forerunner of the Messiah (Luke 1:16–17, 76–79; 3:1–18; cf. Isa. 40:3–5; Mal. 4:5–6). John emerged in a world where ritual washing was common, preaching a baptism of repentance 'for the forgiveness of sins' (Mark 1:4; Luke 3:3).

Precedents for John's baptism
The Old Testament prescribed ritual washing for Israelites in different contexts to express the need for cleansing from sin and contamination (Lev. 13 – 17; Num. 19). Although there is debate about when the practice started, men converting to Judaism from paganism had to go through a form of water baptism, as well as being circumcised and offering a sacrifice.[2] Wives and children were baptized when husbands were initiated in this way.

The Dead Sea Scrolls reveal the beliefs and practices of a sect of Judaism roughly contemporary with John and Jesus. Living in the desert at Qumran, members of this community used many of the washings prescribed in the Old Testament to purify themselves on a regular basis for the service of

---

2. Some date the practice of Jewish proselyte baptism to the first or second centuries BC, but S. McKnight, *A Light Among the Gentiles* (Minneapolis: Fortress, 1991), argues that the practice began at the same time as the Christian rite.

God.[3] They believed they were fulfilling Isaiah 40:3 and preparing for the coming of God to redeem his people. But they recognized the inability of such washings to purify anyone apart from genuine repentance.

Like the Qumran community John demanded an ethical response and used baptism to help people prepare for the coming of God's kingdom. But John's baptism was a one-off event like proselyte baptism, not a repeated ritual like the Qumran washings. In stark contrast with proselyte baptism, however, John offered a baptism to *Jews*, as an expression of repentance and as a means of confessing sin and seeking God's forgiveness (Matt. 3:6; Mark 1:5). His preaching gave baptism the character of a covenant recall or covenant renewal ceremony.

As John sought to prepare people for the coming of the Messiah, he predicted that the mighty one who would come after him would baptize 'with the Holy Spirit and fire' (Matt. 3:11; Mark 1:8; Luke 3:16). As Matthew 3:12 and Luke 3:17 imply, this describes 'the one purgative act of messianic judgement which both repentant and unrepentant would experience, the former as blessing, the latter as destruction'.[4] After his resurrection, Jesus pointed to Pentecost as the occasion when his predicted baptism with the Spirit would occur (Acts 1:4–5). So John's baptism was an anticipatory rite and did not bring people into the full experience of the

3. See *The Manual of Discipline*, 1QS 3:4–9; 6:14–23. The Qumran community and John the Baptist drew upon Old Testament teaching relating repentance to the need for cleansing by God (e.g. Ps. 51:7; Isa. 1:15–16; 4:4; Ezek. 36:25; Zech. 13:1).

4. J. D. G. Dunn, *Baptism in the Holy Spirit* (London: SCM, 1970), p. 11. John's prediction relates to the overall effect of the Messiah's coming on Israel.

promised New Covenant (see Ezek. 36:25–27; Acts 2:38; 19:1–7).[5]

Jesus' baptism by John

John stood on the threshold of the kingdom of God as a forerunner (Matt. 11:9–15), but with Jesus the kingdom actually drew near (Mark 1:15; cf. Matt. 12:28, 'has come upon you'). Jesus' baptism by John marked a decisive moment in history: the beginning of the Messianic Age, when the New Covenant would be inaugurated by the shedding of his blood (Luke 22:20; cf. Jer. 31:31–34).

But it was not water baptism as such that initiated Jesus into his work as Messiah. When he was anointed with the Holy Spirit, God declared that Jesus was his beloved Son, with whom he was well pleased (Matt. 3:16–17; Luke 3:21–22). Echoes of Isaiah 42:1 and 61:1 in this saying suggest that Jesus was being specifically empowered to fulfil the role of the Servant of the Lord.

From that moment on his ministry was characterized by the Spirit's presence and power (Matt. 12:18, 28; Luke 4:18; 11:20; Acts 10:38), and ultimately he suffered to make possible the definitive forgiveness of sins predicted by the prophets (e.g. Isa. 53:1–12; Jer. 31:34; cf. Matt. 26:28; Luke 22:37).

In his baptism Jesus willingly identified with penitent Israelites, to achieve God's righteous plan for their salvation. As the sinless one he dedicated himself to fulfil Isaiah 53 through his own

---

5. The expression translated 'for the forgiveness of sins' (Mark 1:4; Luke 3:3; *eis aphesin hamartiōn*) could be understood to mean that John's baptism was 'with a view to' receiving the definitive forgiveness the Messiah would bring (cf. Mark 2:10; Matt. 26:28).

'baptism' of suffering (Mark 10:38; Luke 12:50). So two meta-phorical uses of the terminology of baptism are found in the Gospels, one relating to Jesus' baptism of suffering, the other relating to the effect of his person and work on others, as he baptized them 'with the Holy Spirit and fire' (Matt. 3:11; Luke 3:16).

Baptism into Christ
Jesus' command to baptize

Jesus' command to baptize 'in the name of the Father and of the Son and of the Holy Spirit' marks the beginning of a new stage in salvation history, with a new understanding of God as Trinity (Matt. 28:18–20). Now that he has been exalted to the Father's right hand, his role as the Son of the Father is to be openly acknowledged and the Holy Spirit can be received by a person's becoming his disciple.

Christian baptism is like John's baptism of repentance in certain respects, but it differs in being explicitly linked with confessing Christ, offering the benefits of the New Covenant and making disciples of all nations. Matthew 28:18–20 suggests the fulfil-ment of promises made to Abraham and the patriarchs about the blessing of Israel and the nations (Gen. 12:2–3; 17:4–8; 22:17–18; cf. Acts 3:25–26).[6] Gentiles share in the benefits of

---

6. The covenantal implications of Christian baptism are also signalled in Acts 2:39 with reference to the promise of 2:38, which is said to be 'for you and your children' (cf. Gen. 13:15; 17:7–9; Acts 13:32–33) and 'for all who are far off' (cf. Isa. 57:19). See also Gal. 3:28–29, after Paul identifies 'the blessing given to Abraham' that comes to the Gentiles through Jesus as 'the promise of the Spirit' (Gal. 3:14).

> Israel's salvation through the death and resurrection of the Servant-Messiah. 'Baptizing' and 'teaching' go together as the way of 'making disciples' of the nations.

In a parallel passage Jesus declares that 'repentance for the forgiveness of sins' is to be preached in his name to all nations and undertakes to send the gift of the Holy Spirit promised by the Father (Luke 24:46–49; cf. John 20:22–23). Water baptism is not mentioned here, but the focus is on the benefits that are offered through baptism in the subsequent narrative of Acts.

Baptism in the name of Jesus

The command to be baptized 'in the name of Jesus Christ' (Acts 2:38) is linked with a call to repent. In the immediate context this involves a radical change of attitude towards Jesus: acknowledging him as Lord and Messiah (2:36; cf. 8:12; 10:48). Like John the Baptist, Peter calls upon his fellow Israelites to be baptized so that their sins may be forgiven (2:38). But he does this with the certainty that definitive forgiveness is now available because of the Messiah's death and resurrection (3:18–19; 5:31; 10:43).

Baptism in the name of Jesus Christ suggests that the person being baptized actually calls upon Jesus as Lord and Messiah, as a way of confessing faith in him. The name of Jesus represents his divine authority and power to grant the blessing of the Spirit and to save people from the coming judgment through the forgiveness of sins (Joel 2:32; cf. Acts 4:12; 5:31; 10:43; 13:38). At the human level, calling upon Jesus as Lord and Messiah is essentially what makes a person a Christian (Rom. 10:9–10).

> Baptism 'in the name of the Father and of the Son and of the
> Holy Spirit' and baptism 'in the name of Jesus Christ' are one
> and the same. Acknowledging Jesus as Lord and Messiah
> effectively means confessing that he is the Son of God, sent
> to be the only Saviour of Israel and the nations. Calling upon
> him to receive the promised Holy Spirit is another way of
> acknowledging his divinity and affirming God as Trinity (see
> Acts 2:33).

Water baptism is closely connected with the bestowal of
the Spirit in the promise of Acts 2:38. But the link cannot be
pressed too strongly since the gift of the Spirit sometimes
precedes and sometimes follows water baptism in other
contexts (8:12, 14–17; 9:17–18; 10:44–48; 19:5–6).[7] The Spirit
draws believers into a new community in Acts, where 'they
devoted themselves to the apostles' teaching and to fellowship,
to the breaking of bread and to prayer' (2:42, explained more
fully in vv. 43–47).

In summary, Christian baptism in Acts has two dimensions.
First, the water represents the cleansing and new life promised
in the gospel. Secondly, baptism provides the opportunity
for a person to repent and turn to Jesus, calling upon him for
the forgiveness he has made possible and seeking the gift of

---

7. R. N. Longenecker, 'The Acts of the Apostles', in F. E. Gaebelein
   (ed.), *The Expositor's Bible Commentary* (Grand Rapids: Zondervan,
   1981), vol. 9, p. 285, suggests that Peter's declaration in Acts
   2:38–39 should be understood as being 'theologically normative
   for the relation in Acts between conversion, water baptism and
   the baptism of the Holy Spirit', whereas later incidents are
   more historically conditioned and should be 'circumstantially
   understood'.

the Holy Spirit. These two dimensions – holding forth the gospel promises and providing an opportunity to grasp hold of them – are brought together when Paul is commanded to 'be baptized and wash your sins away, calling on his name' (Acts 22:16).[8]

Union with Christ in his death and resurrection

Union with Christ in baptism is suggested by its administration 'in the name of Jesus'. Those who call upon his name for salvation express their desire to belong to him and share his life. Paul puts it another way when he says that 'all of you who were baptized into Christ have clothed yourselves with Christ' (Gal. 3:27).

From another perspective, baptism into Christ means being 'baptized into his death' or united with Christ in his death and resurrection (Rom. 6:3–4). It is the way in which we identify with him in his death and resurrection and appropriate the benefits by faith (6:5–11; cf. 2 Cor. 5:14–15). Paul uses such teaching to motivate Christians to godly living (Rom. 6:12–23; Col. 2:11 – 3:4).

> Although some have disputed it, Paul's primary reference in Romans 6:3–4 is to water baptism. However, baptism as such is not the focus of his argument. 'Baptism, rather, functions as shorthand for the conversion experience as a whole. As such, it is the instrument (note the "through" in v. 4) by which we

---

8. G. R. Beasley-Murray, 'Baptism, Wash', *NIDNTT*, vol. 1, p. 148, describes baptism as a divine–human event, in which the benefits of Christ and his saving grace are communicated to those who believe. But he acknowledges that baptism and conversion do not always coincide.

> are put into relationship with the death and burial of Christ.'[9]
> The ultimate basis for Paul's appeal in this chapter is 'not what
> happened when we were baptized but what happened when
> Christ died and rose again'.[10]

Paul subordinates baptism to the preaching of the gospel
in 1 Corinthians 1:13–17. Responding to the divisions in that
church, he asks, 'Were you baptized in the name of Paul?' He
acknowledges that he did, in fact, baptize some of them, but
says, 'Christ did not send me to baptize, but to preach the
gospel'. Baptism takes its significance from the preaching of
the gospel and is essentially an occasion for confessing it and
embracing its promises.

Washing and renewal by the Spirit

The Spirit gives life to those who belong to Christ (Rom.
8:9–11), enabling faith and repentance and producing the
fruit that pleases God (Gal. 5:16–25). Unity among believers
occurs because 'we were all baptized by one Spirit so as
to form one body' (1 Cor. 12:12–13). The parallel clause
'we were all given the one Spirit to drink' implies that
both parts of the verse speak metaphorically about the
common reception of the Spirit in conversion.[11] Paul does

9. D. J. Moo, *The Epistle to the Romans*, NICNT (Grand Rapids: Eerdmans,
   1996), p. 355. Moo denies that baptism is a symbol of dying and rising
   with Christ and insists that 'dying and rising with Christ refers to the
   participation of the believer in the redemptive events themselves'.
10. Ibid. Moo, ibid., pp. 359–367, expands and develops the argument
    summarized on p. 355.
11. See G. D. Fee, *The First Epistle to the Corinthians*, NICNT (Grand
    Rapids: Eerdmans, 1987), pp. 604–606.

not specifically link the gift of the Spirit with water baptism here.

An allusion to water baptism may be intended in Titus 3:5. 'The washing of rebirth and renewal by the Holy Spirit' is a definitive, initiating work of the Spirit of God that is signified in baptism. But, as in 1 Corinthians 6:11 ('you were washed'), and Ephesians 5:26 ('the washing with water through the word'), the cleansing portrayed in baptism and promised in the gospel is what Christ has made possible by his sacrificial death. In conversion the Spirit applies the promise of cleansing to the hearts of believers and makes possible the renewal of their lives. 'Conversion consists negatively of a cleansing and positively of a renewal brought about by the Holy Spirit.'[12]

John 3:5–8 is often related to baptism. Jesus tells Nicodemus:

> no one can enter the kingdom of God unless they are born of water and the Spirit. Flesh gives birth to flesh, but the Spirit gives birth to spirit. You should not be surprised at my saying, 'You must be born again.'

The critical issue here is the need for everyone who wants to experience the resurrection life of God's kingdom to be 'born of the Spirit' (v. 8).[13] Although some have taken 'born of water' to refer to baptism, it is more likely that the whole phrase 'born of water and the Spirit' refers to the spiritual

12. W. D. Mounce, *Pastoral Epistles*, WBC 46 (Nashville: Nelson, 2000), p. 448. Mounce does not believe that Titus 3:5 refers to water baptism at all.

13. The Greek term *anōthen* is translated 'again' by NIV (2011), but could also mean 'from above'. Nicodemus understands Jesus to mean that he must re-enter his mother's womb, but Jesus explains that he needs to be born 'from above' by the operation of the Holy Spirit.

rebirth promised in passages such as Ezekiel 36:25–27 (cf. Isa. 44:3–5).[14]

So there is no ground in these passages for a theology of baptismal regeneration. The Spirit of God does not automatically begin his renewing work through the act of baptism. As the evidence of Acts shows, the Spirit's coming may precede or follow baptism. Some may be Christians for a while before expressing their commitment in baptism. Others may be baptized but not come to experience what baptism truly represents until a later time in their life.

Baptism and the resurrection of Jesus

Applying the cleansing benefits of Christ's sacrifice to the hearts of believers, the Spirit makes them part of the whole re-creative and regenerative work of God that Jesus initiated (2 Cor. 5:17; 1 Pet. 1:3, 23). They become part of the new world or new creation that God is bringing to birth.

Baptism's power to save is specifically linked to the resurrection of Jesus in 1 Peter 3:21–22. This is because God has given us 'new birth into a living hope through the resurrection of Jesus Christ from the dead' (1:3). Believers experience this new birth through the planting of the 'seed' of the gospel in their hearts, which gives life because of Christ's victory (1:23–25). Baptism becomes 'the pledge of a clear conscience toward God' (3:21), which could imply that it is an opportunity to express commitment to the risen Lord and to live faithfully before him.[15]

---

14. See A. J. Köstenberger, *John*, BECNT (Grand Rapids: Baker Academic, 2004), pp. 123–124.

15. The Greek noun *eperōtēma* (1 Pet. 3:21), which is translated 'pledge' by the NIV (2011), can also be rendered 'appeal' (ESV). J. Ramsay Michaels, *1 Peter*, WBC 49 (Waco: Word, 1988), pp. 216–217, argues

The practice of baptism

From this brief survey of New Testament teaching it can be seen that baptism is closely linked to conversion and salvation, though not in any mechanical way. Sometimes it is offered as a means of turning to Christ and sometimes as a public affirmation of repentance and faith already expressed. This diversity suggests the need for a careful assessment of the way baptism is explained and administered in different pastoral situations.

Historically, Christians have been divided over the appropriateness of baptizing infants. Space does not permit a satisfactory treatment of the issue here, but it is noteworthy that household baptisms are mentioned in the New Testament (Acts 16:15, 33; 18:8; 1 Cor. 1:16), possibly following the pattern of Jewish proselyte baptism and including children when present. The earliest explicit reference to the practice outside the New Testament is made by Irenaeus in about AD 180.[16] My own view is that baptizing the children of believing parents is consistent with the theology of baptism I have outlined, especially having regard for the covenantal implications of baptism.[17]

---

that baptism is portrayed by Peter as an appeal to God 'out of a good conscience', understanding a 'good conscience' as 'the product of the Spirit's purifying work in a person's heart on the basis of "obedience" to the Christian gospel' (1 Pet. 1:2).

16. *Against Heresies* 2.22.4. See J. Jeremias, *Infant Baptism in the First Four Centuries* (London: SCM, 1960); K. Aland, *Did the Early Church Baptize Infants?* (London: SCM, 1963); J. Jeremias, *The Origins of Infant Baptism* (London: SCM, 1963).

17. See R. T. Beckwith, 'Infant Baptism: Its Background and Theology', *NIDNTT*, vol. 1, pp. 154–161; and D. Bridge, *The Water that Divides: The Baptism Debate* (Leicester: IVP, 1977; Fearn: Mentor, 1988).

Early Christian beliefs and practices

In the earliest Christian documents outside the New Testament, baptism is simply portrayed as a washing with water in the name of the Father, the Son and the Holy Spirit. This is first illustrated in the description given by Justin Martyr in about AD 150.

'As many as are persuaded and believe that the things are true which are taught by us and said to be true, and undertake to be able to live accordingly, are instructed to pray and to entreat God with fasting, for the remission of their past sins, and we pray and fast with them. Then they are brought by us where there is water, and are born again in the same manner in which we ourselves were born again. For, in the name of God, the Father and Lord of the universe, and of our Saviour Jesus Christ, and of the Holy Spirit, they then receive the washing with water.'[18]

Three traditions regarding the manner of baptism developed in the first few centuries: submersion (total immersion), immersion (part of the candidate's body is submerged and water is poured over the rest), and affusion (water is poured over the head of the candidate).[19] Each of these methods is regarded as being valid. Baptisms were regularly conducted by

18. Justin, *Apology* 1.61 (J. Stephenson [ed.], *A New Eusebius: Documents Illustrative of the History of the Church to A.D. 337* [London: SPCK, 1963], p. 65). Justin clearly understands John 3:5–8 to refer to water baptism.

19. There is no certain reference to baptism by immersion earlier than Tertullian (about AD 200). *Didache* 8.1–3, which probably dates from early in the second century, indicates that affusion was a permissible method where water was unavailable in quantity. See Stephenson, *New Eusebius*, p. 126.

church leaders to provide adequate preparation and facilitate congregational membership. But it was recognized that believers in general could also baptize.

Hippolytus, who was a presbyter of the church in Rome in about 215 and later a bishop, reveals the way baptismal practices soon developed.[20] A complex period of preparation was required before people could be baptized. This involved questions about their lifestyle and reasons for wanting to be baptized, three years of teaching, prayer with the laying on of hands and regular exorcisms.

The baptism began with prayer over the water and a call for each candidate to renounce Satan and all his works. An exorcism and anointing with oil followed. Three questions were put to the candidates concerning belief in God the Father Almighty, Jesus Christ the Son of God, and the Holy Spirit. The second and third questions included affirmations about Jesus, the church and the resurrection of the flesh, as found in the Apostles' Creed. After each question, the candidates responded 'I believe' and were baptized three times.[21]

Learning from the past

The New Testament practice of offering baptism as the immediate way of responding to the preaching of the gospel

---

20. *The Apostolic Tradition of Hippolytus* 15–21. See G. Dix, *The Treatise on the Apostolic Tradition of St. Hippolytus of Rome, Bishop and Martyr* (London: Alban, 1992).

21. Further anointing with oil followed and the bishop laid his hand upon them and prayed for them. Those who were baptized were then invited to pray with the whole church for the first time and to share in the Lord's Supper. Justin, *Apology* 1.65, also records that the newly baptized were immediately invited to share in the Lord's Supper with the whole church.

must still be a valid option in some situations. But many people move gradually towards commitment to Christ and it is important to make sure that they understand what they are doing and are sincere in seeking baptism. Some form of teaching and preparation of candidates seems highly desirable.

However, the elaborate and extended form of preparation outlined by Hippolytus and developed in later contexts suggests the need to make people worthy of baptism. To imply or teach this is a denial of the grace of God. When people have to prove themselves before they find acceptance with God, they show that they do not really understand the gospel and the power of God to transform us through forgiveness and the work of his Spirit. They are bound to lack assurance or to find assurance in their own achievements or in the ceremony of baptism itself.

A baptismal service should be an occasion for preaching the gospel, to remind everyone present of the only basis on which we may have a relationship with God and to put baptism into perspective. It is possible to make too much of the event, especially if it is laden with ritual and given more significance than the New Testament gives it. It is also possible to trivialize baptism by failing to teach about the many dimensions given to it in Scripture and by doing it with little thought or preparation.

Since New Testament times, Christians have either baptized in the context of a regular meeting of God's people or in places where there is abundant water, and then brought the new believers to the church for prayer and a welcome. Although private baptism has been practised under certain circumstances, public baptism testifies to the reception of salvation by those who have turned to Christ and their membership of his body. Baptism has great potential to encourage and unite the church in gratitude and prayer to God.

Calling for each candidate to renounce Satan and all his works is one way of expressing repentance publicly. Again, however, the practice of multiple exorcisms noted by Hippolytus betrays a lack of confidence in God to change hearts and deliver from the power of evil. Baptism should be an occasion for confident prayer that the candidates will truly experience what is offered to them in the gospel and be faithful, fruitful disciples to the end of their lives.

Calling for each candidate to articulate faith in God as Trinity has traditionally been associated with either a series of questions and answers or a recital of the Apostles' Creed. This acknowledges foundational beliefs shared with Christians across the ages and in the contemporary world.[22] However, it is also desirable that people seeking baptism should express publicly their own understanding of the gospel and testify to the way God has brought them to this point of commitment. Sometimes the testimony of those who have nurtured and encouraged these new believers may also be helpfully heard.

---

22. The early Christian practice of baptizing three times in response to the confession of God as Trinity is no more valid than a single washing with water. This is an area where custom may vary without hindering our unity in the act of baptism itself. As already noted, calling upon Jesus as Lord for forgiveness and the Holy Spirit in baptism is another way of expressing baptism in the name of the Trinity.

So baptism in a public context should at least contain the
following elements:

- An explanation of the significance of the event from a
  biblical perspective
- A call for the candidates (or sponsors in the case of infant
  baptism) to express repentance and faith in Christ, either
  through personal testimony or in response to specific
  questions
- Prayer for the candidates to experience what is offered
  to them in the gospel through baptism, and to be faithful,
  fruitful disciples to the end of their lives
- Baptism in the name of the Father and of the Son and of
  the Holy Spirit

Summary

There are metaphorical uses of the terminology of baptism
in the New Testament, as in the expression 'baptized with
the Holy Spirit'. Related words such as 'washed' are used to
describe the effect of believing in the gospel. But water
baptism is clearly portrayed as a means of holding forth the
promises of the gospel and providing those who repent and
believe with the opportunity to receive what is promised or
to affirm their conversion.

In practice, public baptism can be a means of encouraging
and edifying the church. Pastoral wisdom is needed to decide
when candidates have been sufficiently prepared, since it is
possible to obscure the grace of God by requiring people to
reach certain levels of belief and standards of behaviour
before baptizing them. Baptism ought to be practised within
the context of an appropriate 'before and after' pattern of
discipleship and pastoral care.

The simplicity of early Christian baptism was soon lost and it was given a significance beyond New Testament teaching. The challenge for our churches today is to give adequate expression to New Testament teaching in the practice of baptism, neither trivializing nor exaggerating its importance.

Questions for review and reflection

1. What are the similarities and differences between John's baptism and Christian baptism?
2. What does the New Testament teach about being 'baptized with the Holy Spirit'?
3. How has your understanding of baptism been challenged by this chapter?
4. What might be the best way to prepare people for baptism and nurture them as disciples after baptism?

10. THE LORD'S SUPPER

The community meal Paul described as 'the Lord's Supper' (1 Cor. 11:20) has no exact parallel elsewhere in the New Testament. Acts certainly mentions 'the breaking of bread' in the church at Jerusalem (2:42), but the context shows that this was a way of talking about eating together in their homes 'with glad and sincere hearts' (2:46; cf. 20:7, 11). Their meals were not explicitly linked to Jesus' Last Supper, as the Corinthian meal was (1 Cor. 11:23–26).[1] Paul's challenge to the Corinthian practice is based on what he 'received from the Lord' and 'passed on' to them when they were converted. Although he is likely to have taught other churches in the same way, we have no record of this.

---

1. See D. G. Peterson, *The Acts of the Apostles*, PNTC (Grand Rapids: Eerdmans; Nottingham: Apollos, 2009), p. 161. In the second century AD 'the breaking of bread' was used with reference to the Lord's Supper or 'the Eucharist' when it was separated from an actual meal (*Didache* 14.1; Ignatius, *Ephesians* 20.2).

However, Christian documents outside the New Testament soon show that a form of community celebration reflecting the words and actions of Jesus at the Last Supper was common in the second century AD. The word 'eucharist', meaning thanksgiving, came to be associated with these events, which focused on thanking God for the redemption accomplished by the Lord Jesus. The later title 'communion' recalls 1 Corinthians 10:16, where the word translated 'participation' can also be rendered 'communion'. In this chapter I shall generally use the term 'the Lord's Supper'.

As with baptism, the development of Christian thinking and practice concerning the Lord's Supper departed from the simplicity of New Testament teaching. Elaborate rituals and complex theology began to obscure the true significance of this gospel 'meal'. During the Reformation of the sixteenth century there was much debate about the meaning of what by then was called 'the Mass'. The Reformers devised new forms of service to facilitate a more biblical understanding and focus.[2] We shall briefly reflect on these developments as we seek to discern a truly edifying way to obey the command of Jesus to 'do this in remembrance of me' (Luke 22:19; 1 Cor. 11:24–25).

The Last Supper
The Passover context
There are differences of emphasis in the various Gospel accounts, but each one points to the fact that it was in the context of a traditional Passover meal that Jesus enjoyed his

---

2. See J. H. Armstrong and P. E. Engle (eds.), *Understanding Four Views on the Lord's Supper* (Grand Rapids: Zondervan, 2007).

last supper with the disciples.[3] The Passover was an annual celebration of the way in which God had fulfilled his covenant promises in the time of Moses, rescuing Israel from bondage in Egypt in order to establish them as his own distinctive people in the Promised Land (Exod. 12:1–30).

> According to Jewish tradition, the blood of the lambs sacrificed at the time of the exodus had redemptive power and made God's covenant with Abraham operative. When families or groups of friends gathered in Jerusalem to eat the Passover meal, they were reminded in a very personal way of the whole basis of their relationship with God and existence as a people. In time, the Passover also became an occasion for Israelites to express their confidence in a future redemption associated with the coming of the Messiah.[4]

Jesus had a longing to celebrate this final meal with his disciples (Luke 22:15), but he also anticipated celebrating the *fulfilment* of the Passover in the kingdom of God (Matt. 26:29; Mark 14:25; Luke 22:16, 18). He embraced the prophetic hope of an eternal banquet, prepared by God for his people, when the messianic salvation was accomplished (Isa. 25:6–8; cf. Luke

---

3. I. H. Marshall, *Last Supper and Lord's Supper* (Paternoster: Exeter, 1980), pp. 57–75, reviews the arguments for and against the conclusion that the meal was a Passover celebration, and concludes that 'Jesus held a Passover meal earlier than the official Jewish date, and that he was able to do so as the result of calendar differences among the Jews' (p. 75).

4. See J. Jeremias, *The Eucharistic Words of Jesus* (London: SCM, 1966), pp. 225–226, 252–262; Marshall, *Last Supper and Lord's Supper*, pp. 18–29.

14:15; 22:30). Jesus' words at the Last Supper make it clear that his approaching death would accomplish that deliverance and usher in the kingdom.

The Lord's Supper, which has its origin in Jesus' teaching at the Last Supper (1 Cor. 11:23–26), is not itself to be regarded as the fulfilment of the Passover. In some respects the Lord's Supper functions as *a Christian substitute for the Passover*, focusing on Jesus' death, rather than the exodus from Egypt, as the means by which God's people are saved and brought to share in the blessings of the inheritance promised to them.

Jesus himself took the unusual step of accompanying the distribution of the bread and at least one of the Passover cups with his own words of interpretation.[5] In this way the food was presented to the disciples as a sign of his approaching death and of the salvation he would accomplish. Their eating and drinking would be an anticipation and symbolic reception of the benefits to be obtained by his death. 'Jesus uses the grace before and after eating to give his disciples one after another the additional personal assurance that they share in the kingdom because they belong to the many for whom he is about to die.'[6]

> Some commentators interpret the bread word and the cup word differently, since they were separated by the main course of the meal and each saying was meant to be complete in itself. Thus 'this is my body' is taken to refer to Jesus' *person* – the bread broken and distributed is a pledge of his continuing

---

5. We cannot be certain that Jesus identified himself with the Passover lamb at the Last Supper, but that link was soon made by early Christian writers (e.g. 1 Cor. 5:7–8; 1 Pet. 1:18–19).

6. J. Jeremias, 'This Is My Body . . .', *ExpTim* 83 (1972), p. 203.

presence with them – and 'this is my blood' is taken to refer to his *sacrificial death*. However, even though the two sayings were originally separate, 'we must surely grant that Jesus intended the two sayings to be in some way complementary to each other. If, then, the second saying speaks of Jesus' sacrificial death, we should expect something similar to be present in the former saying.'[7]

Most significantly, the cup word speaks of *the inauguration of a new covenant by Jesus' sacrificial death*. In Matthew 26:28 Jesus says, 'This is my blood of the covenant, which is poured out for many for the forgiveness of sins.' 'My blood of the covenant' recalls Exodus 24:8, where the covenant established by God at Mount Sinai was sealed by a blood sacrifice. 'For the forgiveness of sins' recalls the promise of Jeremiah 31:34. The New Covenant link is made even clearer in Luke 22:20 with the words 'This cup is the new covenant in my blood, which is poured out for you' (cf. 1 Cor. 11:25).

Jesus' atoning death re-established God's relationship with Israel on a new basis. After his resurrection, however, Jesus made it clear that 'repentance for the forgiveness of sins' should be 'preached in his name *to all nations*, beginning at Jerusalem' (Luke 24:47). So the blessing of the nations promised to Abraham (Gen. 12:3) came about because renewed Israelites experienced the benefits of the New Covenant through Jesus (Acts 3:25–26) and offered those benefits to Gentiles.

---

7. Marshall, *Last Supper and Lord's Supper*, p. 87.

Eating and drinking at Jesus' table

The command to 'do this in remembrance of me' is found only in Luke 22:19 (after the bread saying) and in 1 Corinthians 11:24–25 (after both sayings).[8] The present tense of the Greek imperative implies the need to go on doing what Jesus commands: eating and drinking in remembrance of him. The cup saying in 1 Corinthians 11:25 even more emphatically indicates a pattern to be followed ('Do this, *whenever* you drink it, in remembrance of me').

Paul further explains the significance of the action when he says, 'whenever you eat *this bread* and drink *this cup*, you proclaim the Lord's death until he comes' (1 Cor. 11:26). 'This bread' and 'this cup' point back to the Last Supper account in the preceding verses. Jesus' words indicate that the focus is to be on the significance of his death, until he returns to consummate God's kingdom plan. Paul's use of the Last Supper narrative implies that there was meant to be a certain formality about the gathering of the Corinthians to eat and drink together. Their meeting was to be influenced by what Jesus said and did.

---

8. The attempt to trace Jesus' exact words and to determine which Gospel form is most primitive is discussed by Jeremias, *Eucharistic Words*, pp. 96–203, and Marshall, *Last Supper and Lord's Supper*, pp. 30–56. Matthew and Mark may have omitted the command to 'do this in remembrance of me' because it did not suit their historical narrative or because the Lord's Supper had already become an established custom in the churches addressed. The original position of the command is probably as in Luke 22:19, and it was 'repeated in Paul's formula for the sake of the parallelism' (I. H. Marshall, *The Gospel of Luke*, NIGTC [Paternoster: Exeter, 1978], p. 804).

> Sometimes the words 'in remembrance of me' are taken to mean 'as a memorial before God', suggesting a ritual to 'remind' God of Jesus' atoning sacrifice.[9] But the Passover was a memorial meal *for Israel's benefit* (Exod. 12:14), even though it was clearly a feast in honour of the Lord. Jesus indicates that believers under the New Covenant should likewise celebrate in the form of a meal the great benefits won for them by their Saviour and do so 'until he comes' (1 Cor. 11:26).

Taking bread, giving thanks to God, breaking and distributing it was the normal method of saying grace and beginning a meal in Jewish culture. Similarly, a host would indicate the formal end of a meal together by taking a cup of wine, giving thanks to God and sharing it with all present. These were not new customs introduced by Jesus and they were certainly not cultic acts to be performed by priestly officials. Nevertheless, by means of a spoken grace, such meals became 'an association under the eyes of God'.[10]

The Last Supper was the climax of a series of meals shared with his disciples and with the religious and moral outcasts of his day. The scribes and Pharisees protested vehemently about this practice (e.g. Matt. 9:10–13; Luke 15:1–2), but Jesus

---

9. E.g. Jeremias, *Eucharistic Words*, p. 255, argues that the meal presents 'the initiated salvation work before God' and disciples 'pray for its consummation'. See the helpful discussion by A. C. Thiselton, *The First Epistle to the Corinthians*, NIGTC (Grand Rapids: Eerdmans; Carlisle: Paternoster, 2000), pp. 878–882.

10. Jeremias, 'This Is My Body', pp. 196–197; *Eucharistic Words*, pp. 232–236. Following the Passover pattern, the expectation might have been that heads of houses or leaders of groups might say the prayers and recite the words about the bread and the wine.

continued to use table fellowship as a means of expressing the forgiveness, acceptance and companionship that belong to the messianic salvation (e.g. Luke 19:5–10). Such meals were an anticipation of the kingdom of God.

At the Last Supper Jesus clarified the significance of eating and drinking together as the community of the Messiah. He did this by means of his words of interpretation, challenging disciples to remember the basis of their relationship in his redemptive death and the certainty of their hope of feasting together in his kingdom.

Jesus as the bread of life

The Gospel of John does not record Jesus' words about the bread and wine at the Last Supper. The foot-washing incident is provided where this might have been expected (John 13:1–17). Jesus' humility and self-sacrificing service proceed from a love for 'his own'. When he washes the feet of his disciples, he prefigures the crucifixion and points to the significance of his death for their service to one another.

Some have argued that Jesus' teaching about eating his flesh and drinking his blood in John 6:51–58 is a substitute for the Last Supper sayings in this Gospel.[11] Although such views are widely held, there are good reasons for challenging them. When 6:51–58 is compared with 6:35, it is clear that 'eating' and 'drinking' Christ are vivid metaphors for *coming* to him and *believing* in him as the bread of life.

When the imagery changes from eating the bread of life (6:48–51b) to eating the flesh of Christ and drinking his blood (6:51c–58), the challenge is to believe in the Son of Man

---

11. E.g. C. K. Barrett, *The Gospel According to St. John* (London: SPCK, 1967), p. 247, argues that the words 'and drink his blood' unmistakably point to 'the eucharist'. Cf. Jeremias, *Eucharistic Words*, pp. 107–108.

who became flesh and blood and was a real human being. At the same time, 'flesh and blood' suggests a sacrificial death: the one who comes down from heaven must give himself in *death* to bring eternal life to the world. Those who want to be raised up at the last day and live with him for ever must come to the crucified Messiah and believe in the necessity of his atoning death for their salvation (see 1:29; 3:14–16; 12:31–3).

An important clue for understanding the figurative nature of the language is given at the end of the discourse. Jesus makes it clear that 'eating' his flesh and 'drinking' his blood will be possible only if the crucified Son of Man ascends to the Father and sends the life-giving Spirit (6:61–63). Those who believe the Spirit-filled *word* about his incarnation and sacrificial death receive the eternal life he makes possible. Eating his flesh and drinking his blood means taking advantage of the benefits of his death by faith.

So should John 6 influence our thinking about the Lord's Supper in any way? We might say that eating and drinking in remembrance of Jesus' death re-enacts that coming to him and believing in him as the crucified Saviour that is foundational to the Christian life. But it is the Spirit, not the elements of bread and wine, who gives life, and he does so 'primarily through the words of Jesus'.[12]

The Lord's Supper at Corinth

Paul's first reference to the communal meal at Corinth is in the context of urging believers not to attend pagan feasts

---

12. J. D. G. Dunn, 'John VI – A Eucharistic Discourse?', *NTS* 17 (1970–71), p. 335.

(10:14–22). The unique relationship shared by Christians with their Lord, and expressed by eating together in his name, makes any association with demon worshippers at idolatrous feasts impossible. Those who engage in such meals are 'participants' with demons (10:20). By implication, those who 'drink the cup of the Lord' and 'have a part in' the 'Lord's table' (10:21) are 'participants' with Christ and express their fellowship with him in the common meal.

Last Supper allusions

The third cup at the Passover, for which God was 'blessed' or 'thanked', was called 'the cup of thanksgiving'.[13] It was this cup that Jesus interpreted as 'the new covenant in my blood' at the conclusion of the Last Supper (11:25). When Paul mentions 'the cup of thanksgiving for which we give thanks' (10:16), it appears that this technical Jewish expression was known and used by the Corinthian Christians in connection with their fellowship meals, suggesting a formal link with the Last Supper.

'The bread that we break' also recalls the language of the Jewish meal (see Acts 2:46; 20:7, 11; 27:35). Eating together, with a focus on Christ's death and its implications for congregational life, is a means of expressing a common participation in the body of Christ. To eat the 'one loaf' (1 Cor. 10:17) is to share with others in 'that company which, through its union

---

13. Jeremias, *Eucharistic Words*, pp. 86–88. Thiselton, *First Epistle to the Corinthians*, pp. 756–761, 871–874, gives evidence for the more general use of the expression 'the cup of blessing' with reference to the final cup at other Jewish meals, but argues that the Passover allusion in 1 Cor. 10 – 11 is clear.

with Christ, has by anticipation entered upon the new age which lies beyond the resurrection'.[14]

> Perhaps the Corinthians began their meal together with a thanksgiving in connection with the breaking of bread and concluded with a thanksgiving over a shared cup of wine. Eating and drinking together in this context was a means of demonstrating a common participation in the benefits of Christ's suffering. 'The Lord's table' (10:21) was not an altar where sacrifice was taking place, but 'a fellowship meal where in the presence of the Spirit they were by faith looking back to the singular sacrifice that had been made and were thus realizing again its benefits in their lives'.[15]

Mention of the cup before the bread in 1 Corinthians 10:16 puts the focus on the benefits for believers of their common participation in Christ's death before turning to the implications for their relationships with one another. Paul's encouragement to recognize their unity in the body of Christ as they eat from one loaf (10:17) prepares for the extended argument in 11:17–34 about divisions in their meetings.

14. C. K. Barrett, *A Commentary on the First Epistle to the Corinthians*, BNTC, 2nd ed. (London: Black, 1971), p. 233. It is possible that Paul intended a reference both to the crucified body of Christ and the body of his people, without confusing those entities. See Thiselton, *First Epistle to the Corinthians*, pp. 764–766.

15. G. D. Fee, *The First Epistle to the Corinthians*, NICNT (Grand Rapids: Eerdmans, 1987), p. 468. Thiselton, *First Epistle to the Corinthians*, p. 763, notes that Christ's death was being presented by Paul as 'the pattern for life and lifestyle' as well as 'the source of redemption'.

Not discerning the body of Christ

The divisions at the Corinthian meal appear to have had a *social dimension*, the 'haves' devouring their own supper and failing to share with the 'have nots' (1 Cor. 11:21), as well as a *theological dimension*: not treating one another as fellow members of Christ.[16] Those with plenty to eat and drink were humiliating those who had nothing and were despising God's church (v. 22). Their behaviour indicated to the apostle that their gathering together as the church was for the worse rather than the better. It was not, in fact, 'the Lord's Supper' they were eating (v. 20)!

> The noun translated 'supper' was used in the Greco-Roman world for the main meal of the day, usually eaten towards evening or at night. The accompanying adjective ordinarily meant 'belonging to the Lord' but may have been understood in this context to mean 'in honour of the Lord'.[17] As long as individuals were preoccupied with consuming their own food and disregarded the needs of others (v. 21), they could not possibly be having a meal in honour of the Lord Jesus.

---

16. B. W. Winter, 'The Lord's Supper at Corinth: An Alternative Reconstruction', *RTR* 37 (1978), pp. 73–82, argues that the division was not so much between rich and poor as between 'the secure' (those guaranteed security, and thus food, by reason of membership of a household) and 'the insecure' (those who had no protection from a patron) in the social structure of Roman Corinth. Thiselton, *First Epistle to the Corinthians*, pp. 860–864, points to other physical and cultural factors that may have contributed to the divisions at the meal.

17. Fee, *First Epistle to the Corinthians*, pp. 539–540. The holding of a meal in honour of a god was common in the Greco-Roman world (see J. Behm, *'deipnon, deipneō'*, *TDNT*, vol. 2, pp. 34–55).

Their coming together 'to eat' (11:33) was for the purpose of sharing a real meal and not for a token or symbolic feast. However, the technical expressions 'the cup of thanksgiving for which we give thanks' and 'the bread that we break' (10:16), in association with Paul's reminder about the tradition concerning the Last Supper (11:23–25), imply that their common meals were to have a special character.

Jesus' teaching and example at the Last Supper should have transformed these Jewish customs for them into expressions of New Covenant theology. In reality, the significance of the Last Supper was being obscured, because they were not reflecting its meaning for their life together. Christ died 'to create a new people for his name, in which the old distinctions based on human fallenness no longer obtain'.[18]

Paul warns the Corinthians of the dire consequences of continuing to eat and drink 'without discerning the body of Christ' (11:27–32), that is, without recognizing the significance of their partnership in the body of Christ. They were to satisfy their personal needs at home if necessary, so that when they met together it might not result in judgment (11:33–34).

The Lord's Supper, which has so often throughout church history been understood as a means of deepening the personal communion of believers with their Lord, is clearly meant to focus the eyes of the participants on *one another* as well as on God. We do not simply meet to have fellowship with God but to minister to one another as we express our common participation in Christ as our Saviour and Lord.[19] Here is an occasion for edifying the church.

---

18. Fee, *First Epistle to the Corinthians*, p. 557. Fee, pp. 562–564, has a helpful discussion of what Paul means by 'not discerning the body of Christ'.

19. See Thiselton, *First Epistle to the Corinthians*, pp. 890–894.

Later beliefs and practices

By the middle of the second century AD Justin Martyr records that Christians in Rome met together each Sunday to hear readings from 'the memoirs of the apostles or the writings of the prophets', to be taught how to respond to the readings, and to pray. Then he describes how bread was brought, and wine with water, 'the president' offered prayers and thanksgivings, and the congregation responded with 'Amen'. The deacons gave a portion of the bread and wine to each of those present and carried away a portion to those who were absent.[20]

Formality and complexity

In Justin's experience, the Lord's Supper was no longer a shared meal, as it had been in Corinth. A more formal celebration of salvation through Christ had developed, with only portions of bread and wine being distributed.[21] The thanksgiving had become so significant that the food was called 'eucharist'. Justin recalled Jesus' words at the Last Supper as he explained how the bread and wine were 'consecrated' or given special significance through thanksgiving.

---

20. Justin, *Apology* 1.65, gives details of a 'eucharist' following a baptism, and 1.67 gives details of a regular Sunday gathering (B. Thompson, *Liturgies of the Western Church* [Cleveland: Collins World, 1962], pp. 3–10).

21. Justin, *Apology* 1.65–67, makes it clear that 'no one is allowed to partake except he is convinced of the truth of our teaching and has received the washing for the forgiveness of his sins and for his regeneration, and so lives as Christ has taught us' (Thompson, *Liturgies of the Western Church*, p. 8).

'We do not receive these things as common bread or common drink; but as Jesus Christ our Saviour, being incarnate by the Word of God, took flesh and blood for our salvation, so also have we been taught that the food over which thanks has been offered by the formula of prayer which comes from him, and from which our flesh and blood are nourished by transformation, is the flesh and blood of that incarnate Jesus.'[22]

Justin briefly indicates what the thanksgiving involved: 'praise and glory to the Father of all, through the name of the Son and Holy Spirit', some recollection of Jesus' words at the Last Supper, and gratitude that 'we have been deemed worthy to receive these things at his hand'. But the president offered up these prayers and thanksgivings 'according to his ability', meaning that he had freedom to do this without being bound by a set pattern of words.

Soon, however, the 'eucharistic prayer' became fixed and more elaborate, as subsequent Christian documents indicate. For example, the so-called *Apostolic Tradition* of Hippolytus reveals that by AD 215 the church in Rome was expressing a theology of sacrifice and transformation through this prayer.[23]

---

22. I have modified the translation by Thompson, *Liturgies of the Western Church*, p. 8, by replacing 'eucharistized' with 'over which thanks has been offered'. Justin, *Apology* 1.66, believes that Jesus' words 'This is my body' and 'This is my blood' give the bread and wine a sacramental identity as 'the flesh and blood of that incarnate Jesus'.

23. Thompson, *Liturgies of the Western Church*, pp. 13–24. Hippolytus indicates that the bishop was not bound to pray according to the text of the eucharistic prayer, but greater regularity was soon established in this regard.

Bread and wine were brought to the ministers to be blessed by the laying on of hands and prayer. The bishop gave thanks for the incarnation and death of the Son of God and recalled the actions and words of Jesus at the Last Supper. The command to 'do this in remembrance of me' was taken to mean that a 'memorial' of his death and resurrection was to be made by offering to God the bread and the cup, for which he had been thanked.[24] Hippolytus then records that the Holy Spirit was asked to come upon the offering of the church and to enable the believers to confirm their faith in truth.

In the liturgy of Hippolytus we see a move towards the theology and practice of the medieval Mass. This gave full expression to the notion of 'eucharistic sacrifice', by requiring that the consecrated bread and wine be offered to God for the benefit of the living and the dead. Transformation of the bread and wine into the body and blood of Christ was said to take place when the priest uttered the words of Jesus spoken at the Last Supper ('This is my body' and 'This is my blood'). The glorified Jesus was said to be present in the form of bread and wine.[25]

Learning from the past

The Protestant Reformers in the sixteenth century argued that the Mass had become a denial of the gospel and was

---

24. Hippolytus, *Apostolic Tradition* 4. Thompson, *Liturgies of the Western Church*, p. 17, points out that the Greek word *anamnēsis*, which is normally translated 'remembrance', is here understood to mean 're-calling' or 'representation'. However, as noted above, the Passover context of the Last Supper suggests that Jesus was inaugurating a memorial meal *for the benefit of his disciples*, not as a memorial offering to God.

25. See Thompson, *Liturgies of the Western Church*, pp. 27–91.

dishonouring to Christ. Teaching about the need for ongoing 'eucharistic sacrifice' obscured the New Testament insistence on the unique sacrifice of Jesus and its eternal effectiveness (see Heb. 2:17–18; 9:11–14, 28; 10:11–14). Teaching about the Mass being a means of achieving merit before God replaced the doctrine of justification by faith alone (see Rom. 3:28 – 4:8). Seeking the presence of Christ in the consecrated bread and wine was a form of idolatry and hindered people from seeing his true glory and worshipping him appropriately (see Rom. 11:33 – 12:3; 1 Cor. 1:18–31).

As well as writing and preaching about the need for change, the Reformers and those who followed them devised new forms of service. As the attempt was made to remove doctrinal confusion, the simplicity and power of New Testament teaching was re-established. The potential for the Lord's Supper to edify the church and proclaim the meaning of Christ's death until he comes was rediscovered. Assurance of salvation was given to believers on the basis of faith in the finished work of Christ.[26]

Whatever the tradition in which we have been nurtured, there are important lessons to be learned from the way Christian thinking about the Lord's Supper developed over the centuries. Here are some questions to consider in relation to the practice of the Lord's Supper in our churches today.

- How clearly does your form of service proclaim the finished work of Christ and the need to go on relying on its benefits for forgiveness and eternal life?

---

26. Thompson, ibid., pp. 95–434, records a range of Protestant liturgies and discusses the various ways in which they sought to give expression to New Testament teaching and differed from one another in doctrinal emphasis.

- To what extent is the focus on thanking God for the gift of his Son, and thus portraying the Lord's Supper as a way of remembering and experiencing his grace?
- In what practical way is the corporate dimension of eating and drinking with gratitude in remembrance of Christ's death acknowledged and expressed?
- What kind of response to God's grace does the service call for?
- How are God's people taught to understand the meaning of the service and prepared to participate?
- Who is excluded from participating in the Lord's Supper and on what grounds?
- What is the role of church leaders in the conduct of the Lord's Supper?

Summary

The Last Supper provided Jesus with an important opportunity to teach his disciples about his approaching death and its significance for their life together. He announced the fulfilment of God's saving plan in the inauguration of the New Covenant by his blood, but spoke also about the ultimate fulfilment of the Passover in the kingdom of God, promising that his disciples would one day eat and drink at his table in his kingdom (Luke 22:29–30). Eating and drinking together in the upper room was a way of affirming their share in all the benefits of the sacrifice he was about to make for them.

Jesus' command to 'do this in remembrance of me' was part of the Last Supper tradition that Paul passed on to the Corinthian Christians. The apostle used the account of Jesus words and actions to challenge and correct the way the Corinthians were holding meals in honour of the Lord. Their disregard for one another was an offence against 'the body and blood of the Lord' (1 Cor. 11:27). They failed to see the profound implications of eating and drinking together as the community that shared the benefits of Christ's once-for-all sacrifice.

By the second century AD the 'suppers' being held in honour of the Lord were more formal, with only portions of bread and wine being distributed by church officials. This took place in the context of a ministry of the word and prayer, with thanksgiving for the salvation won by Christ as a preliminary to eating and drinking. But confusion over the significance of blessing God for this food developed. Notions of priestly ministry associated with the consecration and offering of the bread and wine to God were introduced. Views about the transformation of the bread and wine distorted people's understanding of the way of salvation.

Recovery of the biblical gospel at the time of the Reformation led to the production of new patterns of service, seeking to express New Testament teaching about the Lord's Supper more authentically. But Christians continue to disagree about the best way to understand and do what Jesus commanded. In the face of divergent traditions we need to reflect together more radically on biblical teaching and how it is expressed in our practice today. It is also important to consider the lessons of history and to see how easily biblical teaching can be obscured by our practices and the significance we attach to them.

Questions for review and reflection

1. Why is it important to understand Jesus' words and actions at the Last Supper within the context of the Jewish Passover meal?
2. How can eating 'this bread' and drinking 'this cup' be a way of proclaiming the Lord's death 'until he comes' (1 Cor. 11:26)?

3. In what practical ways might we fail to discern the body of Christ in our practice of the Lord's Supper?

4. What is the most significant thing you have learned about the way the Lord's Supper was understood and practised in the earliest centuries of the Christian era?

EPILOGUE

Nowhere in the New Testament do we find a detailed report of a Christian gathering indicating how different contributions fitted together and in what order. There are guidelines to follow, but there is no prescriptive pattern of service given to us. Prayer, praise and singing are significant ways of engaging with God together and edifying the church. But meeting to hear the Scriptures read and explained, with appropriate exhortation, is central to the biblical view of the assembly. This is so because God calls us into a relationship with himself through the proclamation of his Word and chooses to sustain us in that relationship by the same means.

The Holy Spirit gifts God's people in various ways to minister to one another and take their part in the process of edification. A prophetic ministry of God's Word that speaks to people 'for their strengthening, encouraging and comfort' (1 Cor. 14:3) is essential. But Christians can also 'teach and admonish one another with all wisdom through psalms, hymns and songs from the Spirit' as they sing to God with gratitude in their hearts (Col. 3:16).

If hearing and responding to the ministry of God's Word is such an important feature of what we do together, we have a challenging model to consider in at least one Old Testament passage. This provides an opportunity to review some of the main arguments of this book and to tie some themes together.

Gathering to respond to what God has revealed

Nehemiah 8 – 9 describes an important series of events in the life of the Jewish community immediately after their return from exile in Babylon. When the people had gathered before the Water Gate in Jerusalem, they told Ezra the teacher of the Law to bring out 'the Book of the Law of Moses, which the LORD had commanded for Israel' (Neh. 8:1). So, standing on a high wooden platform, Ezra read it aloud from daybreak till noon, and all the people listened attentively (8:2–4).

The people stood up to listen, presumably as an acknow-ledgment that God was addressing them. As the reading continued, the Levites instructed them, 'giving the meaning so that the people understood what was being read' (Neh. 8:7–8). This corresponded in some measure to the task of biblical exposition in our churches today.

At some stage in this process 'Ezra praised the LORD, the great God; and all the people lifted their hands and responded, "Amen! Amen!" Then they bowed down and worshipped the LORD with their faces to the ground' (Neh. 8:6). Although the people wept as they listened to the words of the Law, Nehemiah encouraged them not to grieve, but to celebrate with food and drink, 'for the joy of the LORD is your strength' (8:9–12). Those responsible for reading and explaining what God had revealed saw the need to lead the people in respond-ing appropriately to God, there and then.

On the second day, when they gathered again to give attention to the words of the Law, they discovered the instruction to keep the Festival of Tabernacles in that month, which they then celebrated with great joy (Neh. 8:13–17; cf. Lev. 23:33–42). Every day for the week of the festival Ezra continued to read from the Book of the Law of God (Neh. 8:18). So the immediate response of praise and humble submission to God in the assembly brought a determination to obey God in their community life beyond that initial gathering.

Confessing sins and praising God

Later in the same month, as the Israelites gathered to hear the Word of God read, 'They stood where they were and read from the Book of the Law of the LORD their God' (Neh. 9:3). Indeed, we are told that they spent a quarter of the day listening to the reading from the Book of the Law and another quarter in confession and in worshipping the Lord. There is a significant balance here between hearing the Word and responding appropriately. Moreover, their response included both confession and worship. Although the last expression could simply mean silent adoration or submission (see Exod. 4:31; Neh. 8:6), the following context suggests that their worship involved standing and praising the Lord (Ezra 9:5).

The Levites led the community in an extended praise of God as creator (9:6) and redeemer (9:7–15). The amazing compassion and mercy of God were acknowledged, even as the sins of Israel were rehearsed (9:16–31). Praise turned to prayer, as God was asked to regard their immediate circumstances and to deliver them from the hardships they were experiencing (9:32–37). The final response of leaders and people was to bind themselves to a written agreement that they would keep the Law and be faithful to God (9:38 – 10:39).

Applying the message to today

There are clearly aspects of these chapters that belong to the situation of Israel under the Old Covenant, so that a point-for-point application to Christian assembling is not appropriate. However, several principles emerge from this passage and give us guidance about the way we should relate to God and to one another as the people of Christ.

First, the public reading of Scripture, with an explanation and application of what is read, should be central to the life of our churches (see 1 Tim. 4:13). There are many ways of doing this, but the essential point is to enable God's people to go on encountering him through the ministry of his Word.

Secondly, the ministry of the Word should be the basis and motivation for prayer, praise and worship, both within the gathering and in expressions of fellowship and service in everyday life. Christian assemblies often begin with prayer and praise, but Nehemiah 8 – 9 shows the importance of this ministry as an extended response to the reading and explanation of Scripture.

Thirdly, genuine praise involves confessing God's character to one another, as he has revealed it to us in his words and deeds. Such confession can be the basis for a realistic acknowledgment of sin and confident petitions for help and deliverance.

Fourthly, celebrating 'the joy of the LORD' with food and drink together is a significant way of expressing Christian fellowship. The Lord's Supper may be a formal way of doing this, as we give thanks for our common participation in the benefits of Christ's sacrifice. But the example of the earliest church points to the value of shared meals for the encouragement and strengthening of Christ's people outside the larger gathering (Acts 2:42–47).

As we encounter God in our ministry to one another, we are dispersed into the world to serve God and bear witness to his kingdom, until we next gather and then finally meet in God's presence with the great multitude depicted in the book of Revelation.

SUGGESTED FURTHER READING

Worship and edification

H. N. Ridderbos, 'The Upbuilding of the Church', in *Paul: An Outline of His Theology* (Grand Rapids: Eerdmans, 1975), pp. 429–486.

D. G. Peterson, *Engaging with God: A Biblical Theology of Worship* (Leicester: Apollos; Downers Grove: InterVarsity Press, 1992).

—— '"Enriched in Every Way": Gifts and Ministries in 1 Corinthians', in B. S. Rosner (ed.), *The Wisdom of the Cross: Exploring 1 Corinthians* (Nottingham: Apollos, 2011), pp. 134–163.

—— 'Together, with Feeling: Corporate Worship and the Emotions', in M. P. Jensen (ed.), *True Feelings: Perspectives on Emotions in Christian Life and Ministry* (Nottingham: Inter-Varsity Press, 2012), pp. 235–253.

M. Volf, 'Worship as Adoration and Action: Reflections on a Christian Way of Being-in-the World', in D. A. Carson (ed.), *Worship: Adoration and Action*, World Evangelical Fellowship (Grand Rapids: Baker; Exeter: Paternoster, 1993), pp. 203–211.

Patterns of service

B. Thompson, *Liturgies of the Western Church* (Cleveland: Collins World, 1962).

D. A. Carson (ed.), *Worship by the Book* (Grand Rapids: Zondervan, 2002).

T. E. Johnson (ed.), *The Conviction of Things Not Seen: Worship and Ministry in the 21st Century* (Grand Rapids: Brazos, 2002).

B. Chapell, *Christ-Centered Worship: Letting the Gospel Shape Our Practice* (Grand Rapids: Baker Academic, 2009).

C. M. Cherry, *The Worship Architect: A Blueprint for Designing Culturally Relevant and Biblically Faithful Services* (Grand Rapids: Baker, 2010).

Preaching

J. R. W. Stott, *I Believe in Preaching* (London: Hodder & Stoughton, 1982); *Between Two Worlds: The Art of Preaching in the Twentieth Century* (Grand Rapids: Eerdmans, 1982).

H. W. Robinson, *Biblical Preaching: The Development and Delivery of Expository Messages*, 2nd ed. (Grand Rapids: Baker, 1993).

G. Goldsworthy, *Preaching the Whole Bible as Christian Scripture: The Application of Biblical Theology to Expository Preaching* (Grand Rapids: Eerdmans; Leicester: Inter-Varsity Press, 2000).

P. Adam, 'Preaching and Biblical Theology', in T. D. Alexander and B. S. Rosner (eds.), *New Dictionary of Biblical Theology* (Leicester: Inter-Varsity Press; Downers Grove: InterVarsity Press, 2000), pp. 104–112.

R. A. Mohler, *He Is Not Silent: Preaching in a Postmodern World* (Chicago: Moody, 2008).

D. G. Peterson, 'Prophetic Preaching in the Book of Acts', in P. A. Barker, R. J. Condie and A. S. Malone (eds.), *Serving God's Words: Windows on Preaching and Ministry* (Nottingham: Inter-Varsity Press, 2011), pp. 53–74.

Prayer, praise and singing

D. A. Carson (ed.), *Teach Us to Pray: Prayer in the Bible and the World*, World Evangelical Fellowship (Grand Rapids: Baker; Exeter: Paternoster, 1990).

A. Wilson-Dickson, *The Story of Christian Music: From Gregorian Chant to Black Gospel, an Authoritative Illustrated Guide to All the Major Traditions of Music for Worship* (Oxford: Lion, 1992).

D. A. Carson, *A Call to Spiritual Reformation: Priorities from Paul and His Prayers* (Grand Rapids: Baker, 1992).

Calvin Institute of Christian Worship, *The Worship Source Book* (Grand Rapids: Baker, 2004).

J. D. Witvliet, *The Biblical Psalms in Christian Worship: A Brief Introduction and Guide to Resources* (Grand Rapids: Eerdmans, 2007).

B. Kauflin, *Worship Matters: Leading Others to Encounter the Greatness of God* (Wheaton: Crossway, 2008).

Baptism and the Lord's Supper

I. H. Marshall, *Last Supper and Lord's Supper* (Paternoster: Exeter, 1980).

D. Bridge, *The Water that Divides: The Baptism Debate* (Leicester: Inter-Varsity Press, 1977; Fearn: Mentor, 1988).

J. H. Armstrong and P. E. Engle (eds.), *Understanding Four Views on the Lord's Supper* (Grand Rapids: Zondervan, 2007).

—— *Understanding Four Views on Baptism* (Grand Rapids: Zondervan, 2009).

INDEX OF SUBJECTS

For more information about IVP
and our publications visit

www.ivpbooks.com

Get regular updates at **ivpbooks.com/signup**
Find us on **facebook.com/ivpbooks**
Follow us on **twitter.com/ivpbookcentre**

Inter-Varsity Press, a company limited by guarantee registered in England and Wales, number 05202650. Registered office IVP Bookcentre, Norton Street, Nottingham NG7 3HR, United Kingdom. Registered charity number 1105757.